Chicago Ghosts

Rachel Brooks

Schiffer Publishing Ltd®

4880 Lower Valley Road • Atglen, PA 19310

Published by Schiffer Publishing Ltd.
4880 Lower Valley Road
Atglen, PA 19310
Phone: (610) 593-1777; Fax: (610) 593-2002
E-mail: Info@schifferbooks.com

For our complete selection of fine books on this and related subjects,
please visit our website at www.schifferbooks.com.
You may also write for a free catalog.

This book may be purchased from the publisher.
Please try your bookstore first.

We are always looking for people to write books on new and related
subjects. If you have an idea for a book,
please contact us at proposals@schifferbooks.com.

Schiffer Publishing's titles are available at special discounts for bulk
purchases for sales promotions or premiums. Special editions, including
personalized covers, corporate imprints, and excerpts can be created
in large quantities for special needs. For more information, contact the
publisher.

Copyright © 2008 by Rachel Brooks
Library of Congress Control Number: 2007935080

Designed by "Sue"
Type set in Bard/NewBskvll BT

ISBN: 978-0-7643-2742-1
Printed in the United States of America

Contents

Dedication

This book is dedicated to Erik and Ashley; as well as Dan, Chris, Liss, and our parents. Each of these individuals has endlessly encouraged me to pursue my passion for writing.

And to my Aunt Karen, who blessed me with the soft sweet scent of roses on Christmas day in Grandma's house several years ago when my heart was heavy with regret because I had not said goodbye.

Acknowledgements

Many thanks to Dinah Roseberry and Schiffer Publishing for giving me my first major book contract.

A huge thank you to my sweetheart Erik for enlightening me on the story of La Llorona, and scaring Ashley and I to death with late night tales of the weeping woman who lost her children.

Thanks also to David and Kevin for accompanying me and Erik on our Cuba Road excursion, even after David's own strange encounter there with the wagon and the laughing child. (And just so we're clear, you two, we're family now, and you're both stuck with me, so don't be surprised if I drag you both out in the middle of the night again on another ghost hunting expedition sometime soon.)

And to my precious little Ashley—thank you for listening while I read my book to you. Thank you for loving it and wanting to hear more. You'll always be my special girl and no matter what your Papi says, La Llorona will never get you because I'll always be here.

Thanks to my brother, Dan, for not laughing at me while writing this book. (I know you don't believe in ghosts, so this was a prime opportunity to scoff at your big sis, but you just let me write instead. And for the record, despite your persistent denial, I still say your house is haunted. So there!)

Thank you to historian David Hinz who helped me research stories for the book, and also shared stories of his own personal experiences with the paranormal.

A million thanks to Christina Matyskela for photographing some of Chicago's haunted hot spots for use in this book. More of Christina's work can be viewed at: http://www.cmp. webhop.net.

Thanks to Lisa Weinberger of Pearly Writes, LLC for getting me this gig. Lisa is located on the web at: http://pearlywrites.com.

Many thanks to all the other Chicago writers and ghost hunters out there who paved the way with their expertise and made researching these stories so much fun.

And last but never least, I sincerely thank God for the ability to read, think, and write.

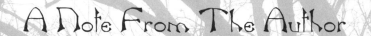

A Note From The Author

If you're afraid of ghosts, then don't read this book. You'll find yourself scared to walk through your own house at night. You might even start seeing dark figures float past in the periphery. Everywhere you go you'll be wondering who's watching you. You'll begin to feel like there are eyes all around you, peering out from the dark recesses of every room in your home. And each night, when you lie in bed trying to fall asleep, every creak and every crack, every unexplained noise, even the faintest barely discernible sound, will have you lying stiff as a board, ears strained listening for more, wondering if you've just heard a ghost.

Do you love the thrill of a spine tingling, hair raising ghost story? Most of us grew up hearing intriguing tales of lingering spirits with unfinished business that can't help but haunt. You might have even gone looking for many of these ghosts at one time or another, but have you ever seen one? Whether you've actually seen a ghost or not, after reading this book you'll feel like they're everywhere—watching you. You'll read all about the most haunted hot spots in and around Chicago and feel like you're right there experiencing the spookiness first hand. It might be best not to read the book alone late at night, though, especially if you don't want to be visited by the legendary La Llorona.

Introduction

I was always intrigued by a good ghost story growing up. I even had a good friend who sincerely believed his own house to be haunted, and I could never resist hearing one of his scary stories. Even in broad daylight, I remember getting goose bumps and feeling a chill run down my spine every time he'd talk of blankets flying off the bed up toward the ceiling and unseen hands choking him in his bed at night. The fascination with ghosts persisted into my teens when I spent many evenings out ghost hunting with friends in the suburbs of Chicago. The fear that infused me on those nights was exhilarating. So when I had the opportunity to write a book about all the greatest ghost stories of the Chicago area, I couldn't wait to get started.

The book begins with several stories of hauntings in downtown Chicago and its outlying areas, including: the Eastland ghosts of Oprah's television studios and possibly Excalibur nightclub, the great Chicago fire of 1871 and the spirits it left behind, as well as the stories of the Iroquois Theater fire, Monk's Castle, the devil baby in Jane Addams' Hull House, and the ghost of Father Peter Muldoon, to name a few.

In the following chapter you'll be introduced to Resurrection Mary, quite possibly the most infamous ghost in all of Chicago. You'll also meet her competition, The Flapper Ghost and an unknown apparition who seems to have a penchant for public transportation. Next you'll read all about the spooki-est cemeteries in the Chicago area, including those of Archer Avenue where Resurrection Mary is known to haunt and the haunted graveyard of Monk's Castle. This chapter will also take you for a walk through Bachelor's Grove Cemetery, quite possibly the most haunted cemetery of all time.

And if, like me, you are intrigued by stories of the glory days when gangsters like Al Capone and John Dillinger ruled, then Chapter Four might prove to be your favorite. You'll read about the supernatural legacy left by these two infamous gangsters. And continuing on the topic of criminals and il-licit activities, you'll also meet the restless spirits of several victims of shocking and unspeakable crimes that devastated the Chicago community, like the Schuessler-Peterson and Grimes Sisters murders. You'll also read about a real life house of horrors, the murder castle of Dr. Henry H. Holmes.

And if, after reading about the horrendous and disturb-ing nature of these crimes and the ghosts left in their wake, you find yourself still thirsty for more, simply turn the page to the next chapter. There, more tales of terror await you as you read all about Chicago's haunted suburban hot spots, in-cluding: Cuba Road, Woodstock's Opera House, the Stickney Mansion of Bull Valley, Palmer House, and several stories of train tracks haunted by tiny spirits trying to lend a helping hand. Finally, you'll read about several spooky legends that will surely send a tingle down your spine, like the legends of La Llorona and El Duende, the Candy Man, the Virgin Mary, Bloody Mary, and even the long standing and entertaining Cub's curse.

Chicago has an extensive history and not all of it has stayed in the past. Ghosts have been wandering around the city since it was established, and even before, when it was still a town. Chicago's ghosts are an inextricable part of the city's fabric. And the people of the city truly embrace them. Some are to be avoided, while others are friendly and benign. Chicago is a city rich in culture, diversity, and paranormal phenomena.

By the time you're through reading this book, you'll know all of Chi-town's greatest supernatural secrets and you might never look at the city the same way again.

Downtown Disturbances

Take an afternoon stroll through downtown Chicago and you'll observe various points of interest including: Navy Pier, Millennium Park, the Sears Tower, the Field Museum, the Museum of Science and Industry, Shedd Aquarium, the Art Institute of Chicago, and many more. On the surface, Chicago seems like any other city—from its towering buildings to its eclectic culture. But what might not be so obvious are its hidden inhabitants. Tales of ghosts and hauntings have always been associated with the wonderful windy city, so much so that many have touted Chicago as the most haunted city in the United States. There's certainly a lot to live up to being called the spookiest city around. But Chicago lives up to its reputation and boasts innumerable haunted hot spots around the city, as well as in outlying areas. So sit back and get ready to be whisked away into the realm of the supernatural as we explore all the greatest ghost stories of Chicago.

Oprah's Ghost

If you've ever watched television or perused the magazines in the grocery checkout line, chances are you've heard of Oprah Winfrey. And if you're from the Chicago area, you might have even seen her or been to a taping of her popular daytime television show. She's known all around the world. She's rich, she's famous, she's got it all; but does that include a ghost? It seems the building in which Oprah's production company, Harpo Studios, is located just might be haunted.

Before Oprah purchased the building that is now home to Harpo Studios, it had served as a production facility to other studios and was even a roller rink at one time. But our story begins back in the early 1900s when the building was used as an armory, known as Chicago's Second Regiment Armory. On an early Saturday morning in the summer of 1915, four ships were set to transport the employees of Western Electric and their families across Lake Michigan for a company picnic in Indiana. One of the four ships was unfortunately not fit for sail. There were more than 2,500 excited people on board the steamer known as the *Eastland*, all looking forward to an enjoyable day picnicking across the lake. A large number of passengers were up on the observation deck leaning over the rails waving at onlookers, putting a lot of additional weight on one side of the boat.

The *Eastland* had barely pulled away from its dock on the Chicago River when it began to list as though it were about to tip over. And then, right there in front of all the onlookers waving goodbye, the ship simply tipped over on its side.

Although the ship was still quite near its dock, hundreds of passengers were trapped inside the vessel and tragically lost their lives. Nearly 850 individuals died on board the *Eastland* that day. After all the survivors were pulled to safety, rescue workers began the distressful undertaking of removing the more than 800 bodies from the ship's interior and the surrounding waters. There were so many victims' bodies, and nowhere to necessarily take them, that a quick decision was made to transport many of them to the nearby armory building on West Washington Boulevard. Workers continued bringing bodies to the armory throughout the day, and it became a makeshift morgue.

So what does all this have to do with Oprah Winfrey? Some say Harpo Studios is haunted by the more than 800 souls who lost their lives aboard the *Eastland* that fateful summer morning. Many believe their souls have lingered in the old armory building all this time. Spirits have been reported to wander the halls. Various Harpo Studios staff members have reported hearing all sorts of unexplained sounds, including: whispers, sobbing, children's laughter, marching, slamming doors, and period music corresponding to the era when the *Eastland* disaster occurred.

Despite hearing all these sounds, there is never anyone in sight who could be the cause of it all, no one except the "Gray Lady." An apparition wearing a long gown and a hat of the style worn by women in the early 1900s has often been seen floating through the halls of Harpo Studios in the evening hours. The woman has been observed in the building by so many individuals on numerous occasions that she has been given the name, the Gray Lady. At one time, security staff even reported seeing her on one of the security cameras. No one knows for certain who the now infamous Gray Lady of Harpo Studios might have been in her day. Perhaps she was always inclined toward celebrity status or the spotlight. In any case, a television studio seems to be the perfect place to spend her days as she has come to enjoy a certain level of notoriety among Chicago residents and Harpo Studios staff.

From armory to roller rink to production studio, the building has had quite a history. Through all these changes what has remained are the stories of supernatural disturbances and occurrences. Harpo Studios seems to have embraced their supernatural friends and has even referenced the "Gray Lady" on the Oprah Winfrey Show website. Tales of ghosts in the old armory building persist, and as far as anyone knows, none of the ghosts have taken up roller skating yet.

Excalibur Nightclub

Excalibur Nightclub has also been rumored to be haunted by ghosts of the *Eastland* disaster. The building that is now home to Chicago's famed club was once host to the Chicago Historical Society. When the *Eastland* disaster occurred in 1915, the bodies of many of the victims were said to have also been brought to the Chicago Historical Society building so that it, too, temporarily served as a makeshift morgue. Some people believe that the ghosts of those victims have been haunting the spot that is now the site of Excalibur Nightclub since the time of the *Eastland* tragedy. While it is widely known that several spirits do, in fact, haunt the Excalibur building, others do not believe the spirits to be those of *Eastland* victims.

The disturbances in the former Chicago Historical Society building have been going on for years and include things like strange cold spots that seem to move about from one spot to another, as well as drinking glasses and bottles breaking on their own. Past and present employees of the building have also reported hearing familiar voices calling their names; the voices of people known to be elsewhere, people known not to be in the Excalibur building at the time.

Other times, staff has heard screams coming from the downstairs restrooms when they are known to be empty and unoccupied. Things are sometimes moved around, and by who, no one knows. The Excalibur's "Dome Room," which serves as a bar, is one of the most haunted spots in the club. Alarms are frequently set off even when no one and no thing is present. The building has had quite a history, which might help account for who some of these unidentified apparitions are. As I mentioned, the building was originally the site of the Chicago Historical Society. What you might *not* know is that it wasn't the first building to stand there. Whatever had been there in the city's early years burned down during the Great Chicago Fire. After reconstruction of the city began, a new structure was eventually erected on that spot.

The Chicago Historical Society occupied the space for a while before relocating to the Lincoln Park area. Various organizations and businesses utilized the building over the years until it became a club, the Limelight. Shortly after opening, employees and patrons of the Limelight began reporting strange events and occurrences that could not be explained. It was at that time when word first got out about the building being haunted. Since then the hauntings have continued, even after the change from the Limelight to the Excalibur.

So what could have caused this place to become haunted? Again, some believe the spirits of those aboard the *Eastland* still linger in what was once a make shift morgue. Still, others believe the spirits of victims of a different tragedy have taken up residence there. During Chicago's Great Fire of 1871, several women are believed to have taken refuge in the building that previously stood on that spot, only to perish when the building burned with the rest of the city. Those women are now believed to haunt the very place in which they thought they'd be safe. One of these women has even been caught on camera. She is known only as the "woman in red." A glimpse of this mysterious lady was captured in a Polaroid shot taken of the Excalibur building several years ago. In the photo, the woman can be seen walking past a window.

Who's to say whether it is victims of the *Eastland* tragedy who haunt the Excalibur or victims of the Great Fire. It could likely be both. But there is a third explanation that might also account for some of the hauntings in the medieval-esque Excalibur building. It seems there was a dispute over the land on which the Excalibur now stands that took place long before the area was really very developed.

A gentleman had been living on the land for quite some time when another man came along claiming the land belonged to him. The two men were unable to resolve the dispute and the second man had the first murdered. The man's remains were left to rot on the very land for which he was killed. A figure can occasionally be observed traveling up and down the stairs at the Excalibur and is believed to be the spirit of that gentleman who was so viciously murdered for his land.

And if there weren't already enough ghosts creeping around the Excalibur, a lawyer, who committed suicide in that location long ago, is also purported to haunt the establishment. The Excalibur seems to have more than its share of ghosts, but it *is* a nightclub after all, and maybe they just enjoy the nightly fiesta.

The Ghosts of O'Hare Airport

We've already met the ghosts of an ill-fated ship that would never reach its destination who haunt the old armory building that is now Harpo Studios, and who might also haunt the Excalibur Nightclub. But the victims of the *Eastland* disaster are not the only crash victims to haunt Chicago. A terrible accident in 1979 killed an entire flight of passengers and crew, who many believe now haunt the area where the plane crashed. The DC-10 had barely gotten down the runway when portions of the plane began falling off, yet it still took off into the air. The air control tower unsuccessfully attempted to contact the plane's pilot. As the plane continued to climb and gain altitude, it began to dip and turn before it started falling apart. As fiery pieces of the plane dropped to the ground, the plane quickly went down not quite a mile from the airport. The plane crashed in an empty field, so damage to the area was minimal, although two people on the ground were killed. Everyone on board the plane died instantly when it crashed. But many who perished on board the plane that day would not go quietly—they still linger at the site of the crash, sometimes approaching residents of the area for help.

Within close proximity to the site of the plane crash is a small trailer park. Shortly after the crash happened all those years ago, people living in the trailer park at the time reported unexplained knocking on their windows and doors. Whenever any of them answered the door or looked out the windows, there was never anyone there. Even passers-by in vehicles observed unusual activity in the empty field. They often saw strange floating lights. The Des Plaines Police Department covered that area at the time and took numerous calls about strange activity in the field. Minutes after receiving reports about floating lights, Des Plaines officers were on the scene. They expected to find trespassers, perhaps carrying flashlights which would explain the floating light phenomenon, but there was never anyone there. The field was always empty.

The strange knocking that residents of the trailer park had heard, just hours after the plane crash, continued for many months afterward. Doorknobs turned as if someone were trying to get in, footsteps could be heard walking around outside when no one was there, cries of agony were heard coming from the empty air field, and dogs frequently growled fiercely at the empty field. Residents were sometimes even approached by people asking for help who would subsequently disappear into thin air. Many trailer park residents became so flustered that they moved.

But even the new residents continue to report many of the same disturbances and have also been approached by apparitions. Several different residents have answered a knock at their door and opened it to meet a gentleman looking for his luggage and needing to make a connecting flight. Before they can help the man he vanishes. And on another occasion, quite recent in fact, a resident of the area encountered an unusual gentleman who smelled badly of burning gasoline. The gentleman inquired about a phone, and as the man pointed in the direction of a pay phone, the strange smelling gentleman disappeared before his eyes. These strange sightings continue even today as area residents occasionally have an unexpected and unearthly visitor come knocking on their doors.

The airport itself seems to have attracted some of the fated flight's ghosts as many people have reported also seeing an apparition inside the airport at the terminal from where the flight departed back in 1979. If you can find the old abandoned field just past O'Hare airport and bordering the trailer park, you'll likely also find some of the ghosts of American Airlines Flight 191.

The Water Tower

A well known landmark in downtown Chicago is the long standing water tower on Michigan Avenue. The gothic water tower was once part of the Chicago waterworks that also included a pumping station, but since the Great Fire of 1871, it has come to stand for much more than just a simple water tower. Much of the city burned to the ground during that historical fire, but amidst all the destruction still stood the limestone water tower.

Since that devastating fire in 1871, the water tower has come to represent the persistence of the city, and perhaps also the persistence of the souls of those who lost their lives in the Great Fire of 1871. Sometimes a dark shadowy figure can be seen looming through the upstairs windows of the water tower. If you look closely, it appears to be the figure of a man who seems to be hanging by his neck. The hanging figure has been observed by Chicago residents, tourists, and even respected police officers. Of course, when anyone attempts to make their way to the upper levels and assist the man, there is no one there. Was he a ghost?

There is a story of a man who was working for the waterworks company at the time when the Great Fire broke out in 1871. He continued to bravely work the pumps while the fire raged all around him, even after all the other workers had already evacuated the waterworks buildings. At some point, it was probably too late for him to escape, as the fire encircled the buildings. The man made his way up the water tower away from the fast approaching blaze to an upper level where he was likely able to see a dismal view of the once great city. Perhaps upon seeing the devastation all around him, he thought himself doomed. Rather than be burned alive in the flames of the Great Fire, the man thought it better to be hanged.

So from an upper floor of the water tower the waterworks employee who had so courageously worked the water pumps until the last possible moment trying to stop the growing inferno, decided to hang himself out of desperation. Once the Great Fire was finally out and much of the city was in ruins, the waterworks tower could be seen still standing tall and unscathed. Unfortunately, the man in the tower had already perished and would never know that amidst the blaze he might still have been safe atop the tower.

Many believe it is the ghost of that man that now haunts the infamous water tower. So the next time you find yourself approaching the corner where Michigan Avenue meets Chicago Avenue, take a moment to look up toward the water tower, and you just might see the dark shadowy figure of a man hanging through one of the windows at the top of the tower.

The Iroquois Theater Fire

From one fire to another, we fast forward to 1903, when the brand new Iroquois Theater caught fire during the winter holidays on December 30th. The opening of the ornate theater was widely anticipated. Featuring white marble walls, intricate woodwork, and elaborate stained glass, the theater was something of a spectacle. Chicagoans could not wait for the theater's grand opening. What's more, the theater was constructed to be virtually fireproof and even boasted an asbestos curtain that, when lowered, sectioned the audience off from both the stage and backstage areas. The curtain was intended to protect spectators from potential electrical fires and other hazards.

The much anticipated Iroquois Theater finally opened its doors to the anxious public and remained in operation for about five full weeks before the unthinkable would occur. The theater was intended to hold approximately 1,600 people, but on that fateful December day there were closer to 2,000 people packed into the Iroquois. With the children on winter break from school, many families opted to attend a matinee performance of *Mr. Bluebeard*. So many spectators were in attendance that many of them had to stand in the aisles as there were not enough seats.

Now while the overcrowded audience squeezed into the auditorium, space backstage was getting a bit constricted as well, with nearly 400 performers and stagehands back there. Despite the crowded conditions, everyone nestled in and looked forward to the show. Things were going smoothly until the second act when something sparked above the stage. Immediately after, some small bits of flaming paper or other materials fell to the stage and spread to some thick velvet curtains. No one moved from their seats though and some of the actors even attempted to calm the audience to prevent mass panic. Everyone believed the situation to be under control. The chaos that would follow was the last thing anyone in that theater had expected or even imagined possible.

A huge fire erupted, and when the crowd tried to flee, they found themselves trapped inside an inferno. The theater had a total of twenty-five exits that should have allowed the building to be emptied within five minutes, but that didn't happen. And that fire resistant asbestos curtain burned without difficulty, further feeding the fast growing flames. To make matters worse, some of the performers and theater staff who were backstage opened some exterior doors, and in their escape, inadvertently fueled the fire when cold winter wind gusts blew inside fanning the flames until they filled the ostentatious auditorium.

The fire raged out of control for a mere thirty minutes or less before being put out by firefighters. Unfortunately, the fire had already claimed the lives of 572 people and left several others severely burned or suffering smoke inhalation. Of those taken to the hospital, many would not make it. In total, 602 people ultimately lost their lives as a result of that fire, 212 of those victims were children.

So what had happened that prevented people from escaping the Iroquois Theater that afternoon? It seems a number of things went wrong. In their haste to rush out of the theater doors, the audience unknowingly trapped themselves inside the auditorium. The various sets of double doors leading into the theater were not so easily opened. Rather than open out, they all opened inward toward the theater's auditorium. When everyone pushed forward toward the doors, those closest to them were pressed up against the doors without enough room to pull the doors open. And with the lights going out during the fire the frantic crowd was unable to notice they were preventing themselves from escaping. In the chaos many people were trampled and surely suffocated under the weight of the crowd, if not from the smoke. Still, others who managed to exit the auditorium found themselves trapped in the stairwells that had been locked by theater staff once the show had started in order to prevent freeloaders from sneaking into the theater for a free show.

For those of you familiar with the layout of Chicago, you know that for every row of buildings lining a street, there is an alleyway running along the back of those buildings. The same was true of the Iroquois Theater. Many of the individuals who had been sitting in an upper balcony of the theater managed to make their way to an exit opening into the alley behind the theater. Unfortunately, because they were exiting from the balcony, the fire escape door was several stories from the ground. Normally that wouldn't be a problem since there would be an emergency set of fire escape stairs leading to the ground. But in this case, there was only a platform leading nowhere. The stairs had never been constructed.

As the frenzied group looked down from the platform, they realized the hopelessness of their situation. In desperation, many of them jumped for their lives but didn't necessarily make it. Others lost their balance and fell hard to the pavement below. Some workers across the alley attempted to assist the rest of the folks stuck atop the platform by stacking ladders and planks. They managed to rescue a few, but many more perished. In the end, a mound of approximately 150 bodies lay in a heap in the alley behind the theater. The alleyway was soon dubbed "Death Alley."

An investigation of the fire would later reveal some very disturbing details. There was no fire alarm in the theater, which severely delayed notification to the fire department that help was needed. A sprinkler system had never been installed as that would have been expensive and would have detracted from the ornate décor of the auditorium. Additionally, the auditorium seats were filled with various flammable fibers, including hemp. On top of that, reports revealed that a couple of rooftop vents, that would have given the smoke somewhere to go, had been nailed shut. Apparently, the vents had not been finished prior to the opening of the Iroquois, and because it was winter, workers didn't want any rain or snow getting inside, so they simply sealed the vents off. Without these vents, the smoke from the fire had no where to go and quickly filled the auditorium, likely suffocating many of those who were trapped inside. Clearly, a number of things went wrong before, during, and after the fire.

Some sources have suggested that the Iroquois Theater fire was the worst single building blaze in American history in terms of total deaths. It is certain many of the victims suffered severely prior to perishing. The dreadful manner in which they died might have left many of them restless in the next life.

The Iroquois Theater building still stands today, although it has since been renovated. People have not forgotten the fire, but what they don't always discuss is the alley behind the theater where all those bodies came to be stacked up one on top of another. It seems the alley does not see much traffic, pedestrian or otherwise. Rumor has it that the spirits of some who lost their lives in the Iroquois Theater fire still linger in "Death Alley." Consequently, most people choose to avoid ever passing through the alley. Of the individuals who have passed through it, many report hearing soft cries emanating from the dark shadowy corners of the building there. Others have even felt hands touching them, as if reaching out for help, but could see no one. There are also unexplained cold areas of the alley that are inconsistent with the surrounding temperature. There is a general feeling of discomfort and unease in the air when walking through "Death Alley," which is why most people choose to avoid it.

Someone unfamiliar with the story of the Iroquois Theater and "Death Alley" might peer down the desolate path and think it very calm and quiet. But don't be fooled. Just because you don't *see* anyone down there, that doesn't mean they can't see you.

The Devil Baby and Hauntings of Hull House

You might have heard of the movie *Rosemary's Baby* staring Mia Farrow. Maybe you've even seen it. The movie tells a twisted tale of devil worshipers and an unsuspecting woman who gives birth to a fiendish baby. The premise for the movie was taken from a book by the same name that would be classified as fiction in any major bookstore. What some might not know is that the book was based on real life events that occurred in Hull House on Halsted & Polk in Chicago. Hull House is commonly referred to as the Jane Addams' Hull

House and has long been linked to supernatural disturbances. The most infamous story associated with Hull House is that of the "Devil Baby," also the inspiration behind *Rosemary's Baby*.

Before the birth of the "Devil Baby," Hull House had already established quite a history for itself. Originally built in 1856 by a Mr. Charles Hull, he and his family lived there for several years until the Great Chicago Fire of 1871. Although the house was not harmed in the fire, the family relocated, as did much of the upper class.

The area surrounding the old Hull house soon experienced major changes as apartment buildings and factories sprouted up all over and immigrant families moved in. Years went by and the old Hull house took on a dilapidated appearance that matched that of the surrounding neighborhoods. The house remained in this condition until a socially conscious young Jane Addams came along with a plan.

She and another woman converted the old mansion into a place of refuge for those in need. Jane Addams' Hull House opened to the community in 1889, offering food, shelter, and education. It became a safe house for many of the destitute and impoverished people of the area. It was not long after the home was in operation that staff and residents alike began experiencing some rather strange phenomenon.

Jane Addams even reported hearing strange sounds during the night. Jane would sometimes wake from the loud sound of someone walking across her bedroom floor, but no one was ever there. Others in the house heard the same thing. Jane eventually switched rooms. Several guests occupied the room over the years and all reported experiencing the same thing. One woman not only heard the unexplained footsteps, but saw a ghostly figure standing near the bed as she lay in it. When she lit a gas lamp, the apparition suddenly vanished from the now-illuminated room. As it turns out, the room once belonged to Mrs. Hull when the Hull family still resided there. She had died in that room and now the old lady seemed eternally bound to the house, despite the rest of the family having left long ago.

After a little digging, Jane Addams discovered that some of the house's previous occupants had also experienced the same strange sounds and could sometimes see the ghost of Mrs. Hull roaming the upper floor of the house. Because of this, they had always kept a bucket full of water at the top of the stairs believing no ghost would attempt to cross over the water. That was their way of keeping some distance between themselves and their phantom friend.

But the hauntings by Mrs. Hull would not be the only odd events to take place at the infamous Hull House. There is another more sinister story that plagues the once pristine mansion. It is the story of a baby born in the likeness of the devil who was hidden away at Hull House, where he could be protected from the gawking eyes of the public.

Who the baby was and where he came from differs depending on who you talk to. In some accounts, he was born unto an Italian couple, in others to an Irish one, and still others to a Jewish couple. The account of the Italian couple is quite interesting because the wife was purported to be a devout Catholic, while the husband was an atheist. The wife eventually became pregnant. During her pregnancy, the woman's husband grew quite volatile one day when he came home to find she had hung a picture of the Virgin Mary over their bed. In an explosive fit of rage, he ripped the picture from the wall and swore he'd rather invite the devil into their home than display a picture of Mother Mary above their bed. The picture was tossed in the trash and disregarded until the baby came.

When the woman gave birth, she and her husband were quite taken aback by the unusual appearance of their newborn son. The fiendish baby had hoof-like feet, a monkey-esque tail, pointed ears, and scaly skin over his entire body. He was even said to have small horns atop his head. And he did not behave like a normal infant. There seemed to be a deviousness about him. The couple could not handle the situation and turned the baby over to the staff of Hull House.

The story is plausible, as the child could have been born with a rare genetic condition or several unusual birth defects that gave him the appearance of a devil. The one detail that does seem strange, however, is that the allegedly atheist husband would reference the devil when he clearly didn't believe in God or the Virgin Mary.

But if you don't like that account of what happened, there are plenty more to choose from.

In the Irish account of that story, a similar baby was born to an Irish woman. In this version of the story, the baby was born with the same features as the baby in the Italian account. But in this account, it is the wife's deceit, and not the husband's blasphemous rage that cursed the couple with the birth of a devil child. The woman purportedly had an affair and subsequently became pregnant, but concealed the affair from her husband letting him believe he was the child's father.

There are several Jewish accounts of the devil baby's birth. Two of my favorites include a father with six girls cursing his wife's seventh pregnancy, saying he'd rather have the devil for a child than another girl, and another father who cursed his own pregnant daughter for marrying a non-Jewish man. The girl's father commented that he'd rather have the devil for a grandson than one that wasn't Jewish.

There are a few other versions as well, and in all accounts, the women each gave birth to a fiendish child after some blasphemous remark was made linking the devil to each of the pregnancies. One final version of the story suggests that a man had committed some heinous crime but never confessed his transgression to his priest or wife. His heavy sin would later manifest itself in the form of the devil when his wife gave birth to their first child.

Various versions of the "Devil Baby" story circulated during Jane Addams' stay in Hull House. Regardless of which version you believed, the one consistency in all the stories was that a bizarre baby was left in the custody of Jane Addams and the Hull House staff. The story continues. The baby was eventually brought to church for baptism, but the baby somehow ran away before the priest could finish the ceremony. The baby became so troublesome that Jane was left with no other alternative than to lock the baby away in the attic of Hull House. The baby remained in the attic until it died.

Hull house is now open to the public as a museum showcasing the important social work once carried out there by Jane Addams and staff. But it seems an even larger legacy, that of the "Devil Baby," has superseded the legacy of Jane Addams and her work. While touring the house, many visitors report feeling an eerie presence they can not explain. Others have observed an unusual face peering down at them from an attic window when standing outside the house. Some people even believe Jane Addams herself now haunts Hull House. If she's there, she's certainly got stiff competition from the "Devil Baby" she once took in as an act of goodwill.

The Irish Castle

The Irish Castle, sometimes called the Givens Mansion, was originally built by Robert Givens back in 1886. He constructed the sizeable home in a similar style as the sprawling estate homes of Ireland where he was born. Givens planned to share the home with his soon to be wife once they were married. But it would never be, as she died before they ever moved in.

The house eventually had many owners. At one point it was even used as a school for girls before being converted to a church. But it was the years during which the home functioned as a school that might have resulted in the subsequent spirit that now haunts the cathedral castle.

The castle is now home to the Beverly Unitarian Church and has been since the 1940s. One winter's evening, a woman cleaning the church ran into a young girl hanging out in one of the many rooms throughout the castle. The woman spoke briefly with the girl, who commented on how much the building had changed since she last lived there as a student, before getting back to work. But as the woman moved on to another room she realized the young girl's comment didn't make sense. The castle had belonged to the church for more than twenty years already and that girl she had just met was far too young to have been a student back in the days when the castle was a school. In fact, the girl was about the age of the students who once attended school there more than twenty years ago.

The woman returned to the room where the girl had been to inquire further as to what she meant by her comment, only the girl was gone. The woman looked throughout the building, but she found no one. Incidentally, all the doors and windows to the building were locked at the time, so it is unlikely anyone just wandered inside. Still, the woman looked out several windows and didn't see anyone. But she did notice a new layer of snow, free of footprints. So where had the girl gone?

Since that first encounter, there have been many more sightings of the young girl, even by the clergy. As sightings increased over the years, inquiring individuals delved into the castle's history and discovered that when it was a school, one of the girl's fell seriously ill and never recovered. She died there back in the 1930s, before the church had purchased the property. For reasons unknown, the girl's presence remained in the building, and the church just happened to inherit her young spirit when it acquired the castle. The church still stands today, and some say you can sometimes catch a glimpse of the girl ghost and even hear mysterious sounds whose origins can never be traced.

Father Facchini Meets Muldoon

The Irish Castle is not the only church to host a haunting. The Roman Catholic parish of St. Charles Borromeo had a feisty phantom of its own for many years. And if not for Father Rocco Facchini finally spilling the beans on this story, the rest of the world might never have known about the intense events that occurred in St. Charles parish over the course of several decades.

When Facchini was still in seminary school, he had heard stories about a Catholic rectory somewhere in Chicago that was haunted by the ghost of an unnamed bishop. Facchini might have found the story amusing, but paid little attention. Years later, after Facchini finished seminary, he asked to be assigned to an Italian church. He was, instead, sent to St. Charles Borromeo parish in Chicago, previously a predominantly Irish community.

Facchini would soon discover, after arriving at his newly assigned parish, that there was no longer much of a following at the once thriving church. Just a few dozen parishioners attended weekly services anymore. There was already a priest in charge there and Facchini was merely there to assist. On the surface, it would seem there might not be much for Facchini to do. How much could really happen in a parish with only a few dozen devotees? Bingo was a popular weekly activity there, at least with the head priest. But for Facchini, bingo was not on his agenda. He would soon be reminded of those long forgotten early musings about a haunted rectory and discover there was much more to St. Charles Borromeo than meets the eye.

On a sultry August night in 1956, Facchini was sleeping soundly when he was suddenly startled awake by a deafening crashing sound that seemed to come from the kitchen below. Facchini felt the walls of his room shudder with the reverberation. The furniture even shook and the lights flickered. If he were on the West Coast, and not in Chicago, Facchini might have thought he was experiencing an earthquake. Facchini regained his bearings and rushed downstairs to the kitchen area where he was soon joined by another priest who also lived in the rectory. They had both heard the same thunderous roar and had expected the kitchen to be in shambles.

What they observed was absolutely nothing. Not a single thing was out of place. The kitchen was in complete order, as was the rest of the rectory. The two priests didn't know what to make of the bizarre sensation they had both just experienced. But that would not be the last of the strange and unusual occurrences in the rectory. Furniture was often heard being moved across the floor, pictures were knocked from the walls regularly, radios blasted on independently and then turned themselves off, doors slammed, and other odd sounds, like rattling chains and moaning, were often heard throughout the rectory during all hours of the day and night. In addition, someone could be heard walking up and down the stairs when no one was actually there. And Facchini was in the habit of keeping the door to his room locked, but often found it unlocked and open upon his return.

Through all of the paranormal happenings, Father Facchini finally came to the conclusion that the rectory was being haunted by one of its former bishops, Peter Muldoon. In time, Facchini befriended Muldoon, as much as anyone can befriend a ghost. Once Facchini knew who was haunting the rectory, he became almost comfortable with the hauntings and the ghost doing them. He might have even enjoyed it a bit.

On one occasion, a fellow priest was visiting the parish when he observed another priest, whom he did not recognize, working in the church office. The priest later asked Facchini who the priest was because they had not been introduced. When Facchini pointed up toward a picture of the rectory's former Father Muldoon, the visiting priest exclaimed, "That's him!" Imagine his surprise when Facchini revealed that Father Muldoon had died decades earlier.

Now recall for a moment that bingo loving priest in charge of St. Charles Borromeo. On another occasion, Muldoon's ghost would taunt that same priest. The huge portrait of Priest Peter Muldoon, from which the visiting Priest had identified him, was actually bolted to a wall in one of the hallways in order to properly secure it so it was not an easy task removing it from the wall. But leave it to Muldoon, a prankster even as a ghost. He removed the heavy portrait from the wall and left it on the floor. When Facchini and the head priest discovered the misplaced portrait, the priest complained to Facchini that Muldoon's ghost was out to get him. And there would be many more pranks and shenanigans to hassle the bingo worshipping priest.

Father Facchini remained at St. Charles Borromeo for a full four years before securing a position in an Italian parish. During the entire time Facchini served in St. Charles, Muldoon continued to haunt the parish. And while Muldoon's antics drove the head priest crazy, Facchini rather enjoyed them. One challenge Facchini would commission himself with was unraveling the mystery of why Father Muldoon haunted the almost forgotten rectory.

Peter Muldoon was initially appointed to St. Charles Borromeo in 1895. At the time the church was quite new and still under construction, so Father Muldoon had some influence in how things were built. Muldoon's influence is especially evident in the design of the church's altar. Muldoon requested the altar be decorated with white marble that had been carved in intricate detail to match the delicate look of Irish lace. Immediately behind the altar, Muldoon had a mausoleum put in place where he intended to be eventually buried upon his death. During Muldoon's service at St. Charles, the church flourished, and could accommodate several thousand parishioners.

But Father Muldoon would not stay. He was transferred to another parish in Rockford, Illinois, where he was made Bishop and where he would remain until his death in 1927.

One request Father Muldoon would make just prior to his death was that, if he could not be buried at St. Charles Borromeo, his Episcopal ring should at least be returned there. Mysteriously, the ring would never arrive, as it somehow disappeared.

Peter Muldoon served at St. Charles during the 1890s and early 1900s. Facchini would not be there until the 1950s, long after Muldoon's death, yet they would both be there together. During that time, Facchini got to know Muldoon and, consequently, has some insight as to why Muldoon really haunted his old parish.

Speculation suggests he wanders the rectory in search of his missing Episcopal ring. Facchini believes the reason is much more complex than simply some missing jewelry. Peter Muldoon was American born, but of Irish descent, and raised in California. During Muldoon's service in Chicago, it seems he suffered some serious slander from his Irish-born counterparts. At the time, there was quite a bit of conflict between the American born Irish priests and those actually born in Ireland. The Irish born priests believed the Catholic Church was best served by "authentic" Irishmen and not these American imposters.

Muldoon took quite a bit of heat during his tenure, particularly for having been from California, a rather liberal state. Facchini believes this scorn, coupled with the horribly ineffective manner in which the rectory was being run in later years, would contribute to the frustration that drove Muldoon to haunt his old rectory. The once flourishing church was finally torn down in 1968, after years of mismanagement.

The site is now a parking garage to the Cook County Juvenile Court. But despite the destruction of St. Charles Borromeo, Facchini felt Muldoon still lingered and followed him from time to time, even after Facchini left the priesthood to be married and have a family. It wasn't until Rocco Facchini decided to write a book about his experiences in the haunted rectory and have it published that Peter Muldoon would finally rest peacefully.

St. Rita's Church

The story of St. Rita's is unique because its haunting was reserved to a single isolated incident, but it was so bizarre that it continues to be told to this day. The unusual episode took place in 1961. It was All Souls Day, November 2nd, and the congregation of St. Rita's Church had gathered in remembrance. It was quiet in the church as the vigil carried on when suddenly, from the loft above the church doors, the organ began to play. The congregation looked up to see who could be playing the organ during the quiet service of remembrance for the dead. What they saw would simultaneously shock and terrify them.

There in the loft were six semi-transparent cloaked figures, three shrouded in black and the other three in white. They surrounded the organ as it continued to play on its own. The parishioners couldn't believe their eyes. In their fright, they all ran for the doors but couldn't escape. The doors were jammed shut. While the congregation stood trapped in the church, they watched as the foreboding figures floated down from the loft to the main floor. The robed figures then drifted over the pews and across the sanctuary to the front of the church. They were heard to say "pray for us," and then a strong gust of wind blew through the church and pushed the doors open. Everyone rushed outside to safety and the figures disappeared, never to be seen again. Of course, the official statement of the church was that no such incident ever occurred, but those who were there know that it happened.

So who were those black and white robed figures? No one has ever been able to figure that out, but on All Souls Day, church members pray for the deceased who have not yet moved on to heaven from purgatory. The belief is that sins are still with us for a while after death and must be purged before moving on to heaven. Parishioners pray for the deceased with the purpose of helping remove the stain of sin so their departed family and friends can enter heaven.

When those six apparitions asked the congregation to pray for them, they must have been hoping to make it to heaven. Perhaps the parishioners listened and said a prayer for the six haunting figures, helping them finally escape purgatory. Since they were never seen in the church again after that night, one can only hope that was the case.

There's Something About Mary

Would you ever pick up a hitchhiker? Most of us have reservations about such good Samaritan acts, especially after hearing horror stories of murderous hitchers in the night—even if only in the movies. But imagine driving down a long road one stormy night with the rain hammering down so hard the wipers can't clear it fast enough. You're feeling more than a little nervous driving in such hazardous conditions, but are relieved to be sitting in the warmth of your vehicle out of the rain.

And then you see her. There is an innocent young woman standing along the side of the road in a white dress, stranded and alone, so you pull over and offer her a ride. Despite being soaked to the bone she is clearly quite breathtaking, with beautiful blonde hair and sparkling blue eyes.

She doesn't say much as you drive along not knowing exactly where you are taking her. She only tells you to continue driving in the same direction you were already traveling when you picked her up. "Stop!" she shouts. You pull over quickly, and she is out before you ever hear the door open or close. You glance in the rearview mirror, and then look out your window wondering where the mysterious young lady could have disappeared to so quickly.

And then a chill runs down your spine when, through the pouring rain, you see a cemetery on the other side of the road. There are no houses, only the cemetery, and the girl is nowhere to be seen.

Resurrection Mary

An experience like the one just described might leave you a bit shaken. You'd probably be asking a million questions. Who was that girl? What was she doing out alone in the rain so late at night? Was she lost? Why did she ask to get out at the cemetery and where did she disappear to after getting out of the car? Was any of that even real? Maybe your mind was playing tricks on you and you only imagined the entire encounter. But after

Resurrection Cemetery, home of Resurrection Mary, Chicago's most famous ghost. *Photo courtesy of Christina Matyskela*

telling friends your strange story, you discover you're not the only one to have met this mysterious girl. It seems she's been seen wandering along the road many other times as well; and almost always asks to be dropped off in front of that same cemetery, Resurrection Cemetery. Her name is Mary, but she has come to be called Resurrection Mary.

Resurrection Mary is quite infamous in the Chicago area. She has been seen by countless witnesses, and has even caught rides with many of them, each time requesting to be dropped off in front of Resurrection Cemetery along Archer Avenue on the south side of the city. Reports of Resurrection Mary first began circulating in the 1930s and have continued through today, with the most prevalent sightings occurring all throughout the 1970s when Resurrection Cemetery was being renovated. Mary hasn't aged since that first sighting back in the thirties, suggesting there is something supernatural about her. This would also explain why she retires to a cemetery every evening and how she is able to virtually vanish into thin air. Resurrection Mary is, in fact, one of Chicago's most well known ghosts.

A Chicago cab driver actually experienced an encounter similar to the scenario described above when he met Mary one chilly December night as he was driving along Archer Avenue. He had just passed the Willowbrook Ballroom when he saw a young woman walking along the road—alone in the rain and sleet. The woman was not wearing a coat, only a white cocktail dress with a tiny shawl wrapped around her shoulders. The cab driver pulled over to offer the girl a ride, no charge.

When he asked where she needed to go, the only instructions she provided were to continue driving down Archer Avenue. The cab driver attempted friendly conversation but the girl remained quiet until she suddenly called out for the driver to stop because she needed to get out. As the compliant cab driver quickly pulled to the side of the road he realized they had stopped in front of a cemetery and told the young woman she shouldn't get out there—but it was

The Willowbrook Ballroom where Resurrection Mary was last seen alive.
Photo courtesy of Christina Matyskela

too late. She was already gone without a sound. Each time
the cab driver recounted his story, he always insisted that he
never heard the doors of the cab open or close. The young
woman simply vanished from the back seat of his cab while
he was parked directly in front of the main gates to Resurrection Cemetery.

That cab driver was not the only individual to offer Mary
a ride. Many other drivers have reported similar experiences,
picking up a young woman along Archer Avenue who suddenly vanishes from the car as they pass by Resurrection Cemetery. And these encounters with Mary are not being reported
by just anyone, as some of those generous enough to offer the
poor girl a ride have included ministers and priests.

Still, other witnesses have observed Mary alongside the road, although, not necessarily walking. She has been seen lying maimed roadside, as if left behind by some hit and run driver. In one particular instance, a female driver spotted Mary lying injured on the side of the road after apparently being hit by another driver. The woman placed a call and police were dispatched to the scene, but when they arrived there was no body to be found. The woman lying alongside the road, presumably Mary, seemed to disappear. As the officers approached the shaken woman who had placed the call they observed an area of indented grass in the shape of a body. The distraught woman claimed there had been a body there, but that it just plain vanished right before her eyes when the squad car pulled up. The officers never did find the body anywhere.

Numerous other accounts of a female hit and run victim lying along the side of the road and subsequently disappearing have been reported, and all are believed to be Resurrection Mary sightings. But if that doesn't send a chill down your spine, imagine being the driver to hit her. Some drivers have had the harrowing experience of nearly hitting Mary, who seems to dart into the road from out of nowhere. Other drivers have even reported actually hitting her. As they were driving along, a woman suddenly seemed to jump in front of their cars.

Always happening so quickly with never enough time to stop, the driver in each instance undoubtedly cringed and tensed up, perhaps even closed his or her eyes, but at the moment of impact, cars always seem to pass right through the woman as she, once again, vanishes into thin air.

On one occasion, as an unsuspecting driver passed by the gates of Resurrection Cemetery, Mary darted in front of his car. Like all the other incidents, his car also passed right through the apparition. This time, instead of simply disappearing, the driver actually saw Mary turn and run right through the closed cemetery gates. In yet another close encounter with Resurrection Mary, a driver hit her somewhere along Archer Avenue. When the driver exited his vehicle to help the poor woman he had just struck down, he was astonished upon not being able to locate her body. The bewildered driver then proceeded to travel a bit further down the road in search of a phone to call for assistance.

He stopped at a nearby lounge and recounted his story to the lounge owner who thought the driver's story sounded sketchy. The lounge owner, Chet Prusinski, was hesitant to buy into the driver's account of what had happened. However, a short time later, another driver stopped by the lounge and shared the very same story. He had seen the first driver hit the woman, who subsequently vanished before either of them could come to her aid. The police were called, and officers went to the scene of the accident, but found nothing. There was no sign of Resurrection Mary. She had vanished once again.

While there is something about Mary, there is also something about that cemetery. Mary seems bound to it, so much so that she left something of a lasting impression. It was a pleasant August night back in 1976, when a driver traveling down Archer Avenue noticed something strange beyond the gates of Resurrection Cemetery. It was somewhere around 10:30 pm as the driver was passing by the cemetery and subsequently observed a woman in white trapped inside. She was clutching the bars of the iron cemetery gate as though she were trying to get out. Nervously, the driver hurried to the Justice police station, not far from Resurrection Cemetery, to report that a woman had been locked in the cemetery. An officer went to the cemetery to help the woman, but when he arrived there was no one in sight. However, what the officer did find would leave an indelible impression on him and anyone else who would hear about it.

Upon being unable to find the trapped girl, the officer looked around for some sign of her and there it was right in front of him. The green colored iron cemetery gate, that the trapped girl had purportedly been seen gripping by the passing driver, was mangled and scorched. Two bars had been bent as though someone or something were trying to escape. Further, those same bars were scorched black and contained visible handprints. Could Resurrection Mary have gripped the bars so tightly in her effort to escape the cemetery that her handprints were scorched directly into the metal? It would seem so.

But that's not the end of it. Once word of this most recent Mary sighting and the evidence she left behind got out, everyone flocked to the cemetery to witness for themselves the twisted and scorched iron bars of the gate bearing Mary's handprints. Caretakers of the cemetery made several attempts to remove Mary's legacy, first by burning the scorched areas with a blowtorch, and then by removing the bent bars altogether. The bars were straightened again and repainted green. But when the bars were put back on the gate in the areas originally scorched, they appeared black once again, and handprints could still be seen. Despite the many endeavors to conceal the black scorch marks or the small feminine handprints, it was to no avail—nothing seemed to work. That indelible impression could not be covered, so the cemetery workers were finally forced to remove the bars from the gate, never to be returned.

So who was this woman we so casually call Resurrection Mary? Is her body buried in Resurrection Cemetery, while her soul refuses to rest in peace? Maybe she wasn't buried there at all. She might have been the victim of a fatal hit and run accident that occurred in front of the cemetery. There are various explanations of who Mary might have been, some of which have been ruled out, while other versions simply don't seem to fit.

There is one account, though, telling of who Mary likely was that is generally accepted among the majority of researchers who have investigated her story over the years. Mary would have been a young woman in the early 1930s. It is believed that she was out enjoying an evening of socializing and dancing with her boyfriend at the popular O'Henry Ballroom located on Archer Avenue in Chicago. Unfortunately, at some point during the festive evening, Mary and her beau quarreled and, despite the frigid winter night, Mary ventured out on her own, leaving her beau and the ballroom behind. Mary's boyfriend did not immediately follow, so she ensued to walk alone along Archer Avenue in the cold winter night air. She had not traveled far when an approaching vehicle hit her. The driver did not stick around to help, but fled the scene, perhaps in fear. Without any immediate assistance, Mary died alone along the side of the road under the dark night sky. It is believed that she was buried by her parents in the nearby Resurrection Cemetery, garbed in a white dress and shoes, much like she might have worn out dancing.

The O'Henry Ballroom on Archer Avenue, where Mary had her last dance, still stands today, but is now called the Willowbrook Ballroom. Why does that name sound familiar? The cabbie who gave Mary a ride that stormy winter night so long ago had picked her up near the Willowbrook Ballroom.

But others have actually met her *inside* the ballroom, and have even danced with her! One gentleman, named Jerry Palus, spent an entire evening with the enchanting Mary at another ballroom, the Liberty Grove and Hall. Palus had attended dances at the Liberty Grove and Hall many times. He had often seen a striking young woman there but had never approached her, until one evening in 1939, when he worked up the courage to ask her to dance. She agreed and they danced off and on over the next several hours. The beautiful young woman was not much for talking and seemed a bit aloof, but she might have just been feeling shy. However, Palus also noted the woman's skin was quite cold to the touch, and again experienced the same cold, clammy sensation when he kissed her lips later that evening, but he dismissed it. Perhaps she was just cold.

During a conversation earlier that evening, the young woman had mentioned where she lived, so when she asked Palus for a ride home after the dance he thought nothing of it. When they got in Palus' car, the young woman asked him to head toward Archer Avenue, which didn't make sense to him because it was out of the way from where the girl had earlier said she lived. She insisted, though, so Palus headed for Archer Avenue. Is this sounding familiar yet?

As you might have guessed, the young woman asked Palus to pull over in front of Resurrection Cemetery, which he did. Palus was quite confused at this point and tried to inquire as to why she needed to get out there. As a gentlemanly gesture, Palus offered to walk the woman across the street, but she declined. She told him she must get out there, and that where she was going, he could not follow. She exited the car and a moment later was gone. She simply disappeared into the night before passing through the gates of the cemetery.

Palus was understandably shaken and could not forget the strange encounter. The very next day he thought to check out the address the young woman had said was her home. An older woman came to the door and Palus asked for the young woman, commenting that he had danced with the older woman's daughter the night before. The woman looked strangely at him and said that was impossible. Her daughter had died several years ago. But inside the house, Palus eyed a family photo and pointed out the very same woman he had just spent an evening with dancing, the same woman that disappeared in front of the gates of Resurrection Cemetery. It was the woman's daughter, and she had died several years prior.

Palus had waltzed with a ghost.

The Flapper Ghost

Mary has charmed rides with many different people over the years who have all commented on her beauty, but it seems she might have some competition? At least two other hitchhiking apparitions have been spotted in the Chicago area as well. The first has been dubbed the "Flapper Ghost" based on her 20s-era attire. In contrast to Mary's fair hair, the Flapper Ghost girl is a brunette and she is always observed to be wearing a flapper dress. She has been spotted around the Jewish Waldheim Cemetery on South Harlem Avenue in Chicago. She is often observed standing near the gates of the cemetery, but has also been spotted hitching rides along nearby Des Plaines Avenue.

The Melody Mill Ballroom used to be located on Des Plaines Avenue and some say the hitchhiking flapper girl was a young Jewish woman who used to dance in that ballroom so many years ago. Sounds a lot like the story of Resurrection Mary doesn't it? Unlike Mary, though, the flapper girl seems to be a bit more talkative. Anytime someone has been nice enough to give her a ride home from the ballroom, she always explains how she lives in the caretaker's house at the Waldheim Cemetery. That's reasonable enough to prevent her escorts from wondering why she would want to be dropped off in front of a cemetery. Although, each time a young man has dropped her off, she always seems to suddenly disappear from sight as she passes by the headstones of the graves over which she walks.

One evening a policeman even gave the girl a ride home. It was a rainy night in 1979, and the girl happened to be walking alone past the Melody Mill Ballroom. The officer kindly offered her a ride home, so she got in and instructed him to drop her off at an apartment building right by the Waldheim Cemetery. The officer was perplexed when the girl seemed to disappear near the building after getting out of the car. He thought something might have happened to her, as there was no possible way she had gotten inside the building that quickly. He walked over to the covered entryway of the building where the girl had virtually vanished. To his amazement the covered walkway was bone dry, not a single wet footprint was visible despite the rainy conditions. The girl could not possibly have entered the building here, so where did she go?

Now before you think these lovely young hitchhiking ghosts only make appearances during the evening hours, it might be a good time to tell you about a daytime sighting of the Flapper Ghost. The year 1973 seems to have been a good one for the Flapper Ghost when she was often seen at the Melody Mill Ballroom. However, she made a surprise appearance in broad daylight one afternoon. She was spotted by an entire family at the Jewish Waldheim Cemetery. While the family was paying their respects, they saw a striking young woman unusually dressed like someone from the flapper era walking around near a crypt—when she suddenly vanished from sight.

They were all a bit startled by the young woman's instant and unexplained disappearance, and they rushed over to the crypt area to have a look. But there was nothing to see. The woman was gone. The interesting thing about that sighting at the crypt is that several other passers by have seen a young woman resembling the Flapper Ghost enter a crypt or mausoleum-type structure on various occasions while driving by the cemetery.

Resurrection Mary and the Flapper Ghost are not alone, as there have been sightings of a third hitchhiking female apparition. This hitcher seems to be a bit younger than her slightly more mature counterparts and is believed by many to have been a young teen who was buried in Evergreen Cemetery. The interesting thing about her is that she seems to venture further from her cemetery than either Mary or the flapper girl ever has.

A mass of sightings occurred throughout the 1980s, when the young teen was frequently picked up by motorists in both the southern and western suburbs of Chicago, not necessarily near the Evergreen Cemetery in Evergreen Park. The girl always asks for a ride to the cemetery though. And like both Resurrection Mary and the Flapper Ghost, the young hitcher also seems to vanish into thin air upon arriving back at the cemetery.

But sightings of this adolescent apparition are not limited to hitchhiking encounters alone. The young teen has also been spotted waiting at the bus stop just across the street from Evergreen Cemetery, and sometimes even hops on board without paying. On one occasion, a bus driver, frustrated by the girl's non responsiveness when asked to pay the fare, got up before continuing on his route and walked back to collect the girl's money. Only he would not be able to collect this fare, because when he approached the teen, she vanished into thin air. Countless others have reported witnessing this same vanishing act while waiting for the bus at the stop across the street from the Evergreen Cemetery. So what's with all the vanishing hitchhikers in Chicago? No one knows for sure, but my bet is that if you were a ghost who'd strayed too far from your cemetery, you just might hitch a ride home too.

The Other Mary

Resurrection Mary is certainly the most infamous of Chi-town's hitchhiking apparitions, and possibly the most popular ghost in all of Chicago, but there's another ghost who shares her namesake. This other Mary haunts the halls of Pemberton Hall, one of the women's dorms on the Eastern Illinois University campus in Charleston, Illinois. Unlike her classmates, Mary Hawkins, once a student at Eastern and resident of Pemberton Hall, would never graduate. In fact, she would never leave the campus. Her benevolent spirit is always around looking after the residents of Pemberton Hall. Girls who go to sleep leaving their dorm room doors unlocked, wake in the morning to find someone's locked the door for them during the night. Lights, televisions, and radios left on are often turned off by her as well. Although, in the wake of the subsequent silence when everything has been turned off, other unexplained noises become readily audible, such as knocking and scratching sounds on the doors and walls. And sometimes the faint sound of a piano being played can be heard coming from the fourth floor of the dorm, a floor that has long been closed off without inhabitants.

So what could have happened in Pemberton Hall to cause the spirit of Mary Hawkins to linger indefinitely? Sometime back in 1917, on a nasty winter night, one of the college co-eds was having a hard time sleeping. Her restlessness prompted her to exit her dorm room and wander down to the music room where she took a seat at the piano and began playing quietly, as the hour was late. While the unsuspecting young woman continued to tickle the ivory keys of the piano, a sinister event was unfolding. A male janitor with keys to the building had let himself in and made his way up to the fourth floor where the insomnia plagued girl played the piano. As the girl's fingers danced across the smooth white keys, she was grabbed from behind by the janitor, who violently beat her to a bloody pulp, sexually assaulted her, and left her for dead before escaping into the dark veil of night. The tenacious young woman roused enough strength to pull herself along the floor, out of the music room, and down the hall to the stairwell. She made it down the stairs leaving a bloody trail behind her and, with the little bit of strength she had left, began scratching at the dorm room doors of her fellow Pemberton Hall residents, but no one woke to help her. Her cold dead body would be found immediately outside the door of the resident advisor's room. The girl died alone and in agony. But the girl was not Mary Hawkins.

The identity of that girl seems to have died with her because in all the tales of the Pemberton Hall hauntings, the murdered girl's name is never said. And while many believe the murdered pianist does sometimes haunt the dorm, most hauntings are attributed to Mary Hawkins.

So who was Mary Hawkins? Remember that resident advisor's door, the one in front of which the slain girl ultimately died? As you might have guessed, the resident advisor was none other than Mary Hawkins. After discovering the dead girl's body, Mary reportedly felt terribly guilty on several counts. She had not waken to assist the assaulted girl when she had attempted to scratch at Mary's door, and beyond that, Mary had failed to protect the girl from ever experiencing that brutal attack in the first place. Apparently, Mary was so distraught over the entire experience that she soon began suffering from insomnia herself. Other girls in the dorm regularly observed Mary pacing the halls all night long. Mary was experiencing horrible nightmares and ultimately delved into such a deep depression that she had to be hospitalized. She never recovered. Instead, Mary sank into such an abyss of despair until she could no longer stand it and she killed herself.

Unfortunately, death has not alleviated Mary of her guilt over the murder of one of her resident's as she has chosen to return to Pemberton Hall where she now watches over everyone fortunate or unfortunate enough to live there. Unlike Resurrection Mary, this Mary took her own life; however, both girls seem to be destined to walk this world for eternity, long after each one should have departed.

Corpses on Campus

Mary Hawkins is not the only ghost to haunt a college campus. Many of Illinois' colleges and universities are known to have their own eerie occurrences, especially in the dorms and often in fraternity and sorority houses. There is not much to many of the stories, other than some strange sounds and missing objects on occasion, but they are interesting nonetheless. One of the most interesting, by far, is the story of Beecher

Hall on the Illinois College campus in Jacksonville, as told by author Troy Taylor. Illinois College is often touted as one of the most haunted colleges in the entire Midwestern area, which is certainly possible when you consider all the buildings on campus that are purported to be haunted, including: Sturtevant Hall, Beecher Hall, the David A. Smith house, Whipple Hall, Ellis Hall, and Fayerweather House, to name a few. My favorite haunting is that of Beecher Hall, not so much for the actual hauntings that occur there, but for the explanation of how the building came to be haunted.

Beecher Hall has stood proudly on campus since 1829 and currently functions as a meeting hall for a few fraternal organizations. Nothing too chilling has been reported there, mainly just unexplained footsteps walking about from one room to another. Of course, there is never anyone actually walking about when the footsteps are heard so they are most definitely of an unearthly origin. But who is it that might be lingering in Beecher Hall?

It seems Beecher Hall was once used for medical purposes long before it was a meeting hall. At the time, cadavers had been stored on the upper floor. But were they supposed to be there? Many attribute the first instances of "body snatching" to the med students of Illinois College who allegedly stole corpses from nearby hospitals, and sometimes cemeteries, and stashed them in Beecher Hall to be used for study purposes. The body snatching endeavors persisted until repugnant odors began emanating from the house and the overzealous med students were stopped. No more body snatching and storing. The removal of the cadavers from the house might have eliminated the foul stench, but something else was left behind. Perhaps the stolen corpses didn't appreciate the free room and board in Beecher Hall while they were stashed on the upper floor. The footsteps of many of them can still be heard pacing about.

Spooky Cemeteries

If you were raised in Chicago or one of its surrounding suburbs, you might have played the game *Ghost in the Graveyard* growing up. It was always played after dark and one person hid in the graveyard, which was really someone's backyard, while the rest of you looked for your phantom friend. When one of you spotted that friend, you yelled out "ghost in the graveyard" and everyone went running to the designated safe zone. Whenever someone was caught by the ghost, they also became a ghost and helped tag the rest of you. The last person to be tagged became the next ghost in the graveyard.

That game was a lot of fun, and was even a little spooky since it was played in the dark. But ghost hunting is not just for kids. Tons of teens and adults still embrace any opportunity to observe an apparition. Cemeteries are an obvious choice for hunting ghosts and over the years stories of supernatural sightings in the various Chicagoland graveyards have sparked the interest of novice and veteran ghost hunters alike.

Bachelor's Grove Cemetery

In a Chicago suburb, at the edge of the Rubio Woods Forest Preserve, stands a small cemetery that has not been in use for years. In fact, the cemetery was officially closed back in 1965. But despite the lack of activity, the cemetery seems to be a place of unrest. Countless stories of ghostly encounters and strange sightings in the cemetery have been circulating for years. The cemetery is believed, by many, to be one of the most haunted

places in the Chicago area. It is known as Bachelor's Grove Cemetery and it is a ghost hunter's paradise.

There have been many supernatural stories surrounding Bachelor's Grove Cemetery, but by far the most intriguing is that of the "White Lady" or the "Madonna" of Bachelor's Grove as some like to call her. She was a young mother buried in the cemetery next to her infant son. There are no specific details available about who she was, whether she died during delivery or sometime after her newborn baby boy passed on, and no one seems to know how or why her baby died. But

The abandoned Bachelor's Grove Cemetery. *Photo courtesy of Christina Matyskela*

far more interesting than who she might have been in life, is who she has become in death.

The wandering "Madonna" has been seen strolling through the cemetery carrying her baby beneath the soft glow of a full moon. Better yet, her image has actually been captured on film. A woman was exploring the old cemetery one day, casually snapping photographs of tombstones and other points of interest. While there, the woman never noticed anything unusual. No ghosts appeared and nothing mysterious or supernatural occurred, although she *was* there during broad daylight. Perhaps a moonlit stroll would have revealed some of the cemetery's supernatural inhabitants. Regardless, the woman took a few more photos and finished her inspection of the site. She was gone before dark. And although she didn't experience anything spooky or observe any apparitions, she would soon discover she had not necessarily been alone in the cemetery that day.

After the pictures she had taken were developed, the woman was astounded to see a woman dressed in white and sitting on a tombstone appear in one of the photos. There hadn't been any woman anywhere in the cemetery when she was there looking around, and there certainly hadn't been anyone sitting atop that tombstone when she snapped the picture.

So who was that woman and where did she come from? Many people believe the woman in white to be the very same one who has been seen carrying her baby by the moonlight, the Madonna of Bachelor's Grove. Whoever she is, her photo has baffled even the best photo experts and remains unexplained to this day.

But that's not the end of the story. There are plenty more accounts of apparitions and supernatural sightings in Bachelor's Grove Cemetery. Even the nearby pond and gravel path leading to the old cemetery are purported to be haunted. As you walk along the path on your way to the cemetery you can sometimes see a quaint white house with pillars lining the front porch and a gentle light glowing

The haunted path leading to Bachelor's Grove Cemetery. *Photo courtesy of Christina Matyskela*

through the front window as a porch swing rocks in the breeze.

But if you choose to approach the house, it's best not to blink or you might miss it. That's right. The house is likely to disappear before your very eyes, as has been the case each and every time the house has been spotted by observers. The charming house seemingly appears abruptly, and disappears just as suddenly. You might wonder if you didn't simply imagine the entire thing, but sightings of this mysterious house have been reported countless times by just as many individuals, each describing the house in identical detail. However, despite thorough research, no one has been able to confirm whether a similar house has ever existed in that location.

The haunted pond of Bachelor's Grove Cemetery. *Photo courtesy of Christina Matyskela*

There is another story involving the pond on the other side of the cemetery that might shed some light on who might have lived in that house at one time. In addition to sightings of the White Lady or Madonna of Bachelor's Grove and the vanishing house, an old farmer has also been seen with a horse pulling a plow as though he were still farming—despite the absence of any farm. This farmer was observed with his horse and plow by two forest rangers in the late 1900s. Interestingly, there was a farmer from that same area who died sometime during the 1870s, more than 100 years earlier. He had been out working the land with his horse drawn plow when the horse, for reasons unknown, waded into the pond that bordered the once active Bachelor's Grove Cemetery. Once immersed in water, the heavy plow quickly began to sink to the bottom of the pond, forcing the farmer and his horse down with it. The unfortunate farmer met his fate that day and drowned next to his horse beneath the weight of the plow, but can still be seen plowing his phantom fields. And who knows, perhaps the disappearing house seen along the cemetery trail is not just a random phantom phenomenon, but was also the old farmer's home at one time.

There have been plenty more tales of dancing lights, strange sounds, and unusual apparitions told about the trail,

Headstone in Bachelor's Grove Cemetery. *Photo courtesy of Christina Matyskela*

Large tombstone in Bachelor's Grove Cemetery. *Photo courtesy of Christina Matyskela*

Old tombstone depicting some of the vandalism that has plagued Bachelor's Grove Cemetery over the years. *Photo courtesy of Christina Matyskela*

cemetery, and pond. For instance, there have been reports of figures dressed in monk's robes floating through the cemetery on several occasions. On another occasion, witnesses observed a man in the cemetery who had a distinctly yellow glow about him.

And that pond has been the center of some very serious speculation involving the dumping of bodies there by Chicago gangsters years ago. It's isolated and discrete location next to Bachelor's Grove Cemetery would have made it the perfect place for drowning evidence. The desolate location of the cemetery and pond could have also contributed to the extensive vandalism that ultimately forced the closing of the cemetery. Since the cemetery is located at the end of a long lonely trail, desecraters could easily disturb the cemetery, stealing and toppling over tombstones, without much risk of being caught in the act.

The disheveled state of the cemetery became so problematic that Bachelor's Grove Cemetery was ultimately closed in 1965. Not only has the cemetery largely been abandoned since that time, it has literally been bypassed by road construction that cut off access to the cemetery trail from the major roads around there. This might be for the best, though, considering all the ghosts in the graveyard who seem to enjoy coming out to play in the absence of regular human activity.

Monks' Castle and the Cemeteries of Archer Avenue

Remember Resurrection Mary, always seen walking along Archer Avenue on her way home to Resurrection Cemetery? Well there's more to Archer Avenue than just Resurrection Mary. Resurrection Cemetery is not the only cemetery to reside along this spooky stretch of roadway. Archer Avenue is also host to the Archer Woods Cemetery, as well as the St. James–Sag Cemetery. There aren't a lot of documented stories of supernatural occurrences at the Archer Woods Cemetery, but there is a particular tale of a woman in white that has been shared by many residents of the area. It is at the main entrance to Archer Woods Cemetery, which is actually located along Kean Road, where the tale begins.

On many a dark night, travelers passing by the cemetery have reported hearing the sad sounds of someone crying beyond the cemetery gates. Those curious enough to brave stepping up to the cemetery gate often witness something unforgettable. There on the other side of the cemetery gates is a woman wearing a white dress and hands covering her face as she strolls through the cemetery sobbing.

A woman in white trapped in a cemetery at night sounds a bit reminiscent of Resurrection Mary, although this phantom

Archer Woods Cemetery. *Photo courtesy of Christina Matyskela*

female has yet to hitch a ride anywhere. And unlike Resurrection Mary, no one has been able to properly identify who this spirit was in life. So for now, she might simply be thought of as the weeping woman in white of Archer Woods Cemetery.

Not to be outdone, the St. James-Sag Cemetery has its own inexplicable woman in white wandering the graveyard grounds that sit next to the St. James-Sag Church. Little is known about this unidentified apparition, other than she might have been haunting the area since before Resurrection Mary's first appearance in the 1930s. But her story is not nearly the most fascinating or peculiar of the various supernatural sightings surrounding St. James-Sag. The cemetery has long been associated with stories of phantom monks who

Monk's Castle and its adjoining cemetery. *Photo courtesy of Christina Matyskela*

gracefully glide through the cemetery as if floating on air. For years, stories of these mysterious monks circulated and gave rise to other rumors. For instance, it was always unwise to wander in the area after dark lest the monks lay hold of you and compel you to kneel in repentant prayer all night. As similar stories of encounters with the monks perpetuated over the years, the nickname "Monk's Castle" was bestowed upon the St. James-Sag church and cemetery.

Despite it's charming nickname, most people in the area simply disregarded the tales of mystical monks as urban legend. But that was before an officer became involved in a foot chase through the cemetery with the monks. It was November 1977, just before the Thanksgiving holiday. A Cook County police officer was patrolling the area near the St. James-Sag grounds. It was a few hours past midnight when the officer noticed movement in the cemetery just as he was about to pass by. The officer exited his vehicle and spotted eight or nine dark figures wearing monk's robes trespassing among the cemetery tombstones. The officer called out to the unidentified individuals, ordering them to approach his vehicle, but his commands were ignored. The officer then proceeded to ascend the slight hillside and approach the cloaked figures himself, gun in hand. The mysterious monks ran and the officer gave chase. But in the dark, it was difficult to navigate the hilly tombstone-covered terrain. Despite his best efforts at pursuit, the hooded monks passed right over the bumpy ground with speed and ease before disappearing into the night just as the officer had finally gained ground on them.

A subsequent police investigation during daylight hours revealed no clues as to who those mysterious cloaked figures might have been; not even a single footprint could be found. Without any plausible explanation, the officer found himself even more mystified and eventually came to the conclusion that he had been among ghosts that evening.

And he's not the only one. A similar encounter occurred in the mid 1980s, when a group of teens thought it would be fun to explore the cemetery by night. While wandering around the cemetery, a few of the teens noticed some dark figures in the wooded area just beyond the cemetery. What was distinctly unusual about these dark hooded figures was their piercing red eyes glowing from beneath their cloaks. The frightened teens ran for the cemetery gates as quickly as possible. But just when they thought they were all safe outside the cemetery gate, and one young female sat down on the curb to catch her breath, one of those mysterious monks grabbed her and dragged her away—never to be heard from again. What's even more eerie is that there is no record of monks ever inhabiting that particular piece of land. But that hasn't slowed down sightings of these strange figures that can, on just the right night, be sometimes heard chanting their prayers in Latin.

Brace yourself because there's more than just a few phantom monks haunting this sacred place. Back in 1897, the Chicago Tribune ran a story about a seemingly supernatural sighting there. Two musicians had performed in one of the buildings of St. James-Sag late into the night. Rather than travel at such a late hour, they opted to stay the night in the building, which sat down the hill from the rectory building. At about two in the morning, both gentlemen were awakened by the clopping of horse hooves against the ground. The two men quickly rushed to a window and looked out to see a horse drawn carriage approaching St. James-Sag along the gravel road leading up to it, the very road that is now Archer Avenue. The peculiar black carriage was being pulled by several black horses. The carriage stopped at the entrance to the St. James-Sag grounds, marked by an overhead archway. An unknown woman wearing a white robe stepped into the black carriage. But as the horse drawn carriage passed through the archway heading back in the direction from which it had originally come, the entire carriage, horses and all, simply vanished before both musicians' eyes, as though it were never there.

Other similar sightings have occurred on Kean Road near the Archer Woods Cemetery, which is not far from the St. James-Sag cemetery and church. Witnesses there have also

The main gate to Monk's Castle (i.e., St. James-Sag). Visible in the background is the archway through which the mysterious black carriage passed and vanished back in 1897. *Photo courtesy of Christina Matyskela*

described seeing a black horse drawn carriage being pulled by black horses, and the carriage seems to be carrying a child-sized coffin. Could this be the same disappearing carriage also seen by the two musicians at St. James-Sag? Given the close proximity of the two locations, it seems quite likely that it is. Additionally, there have been reports of a ghostly black stallion sauntering among the tombstones of the St. James-Sag cemetery by night, as well as strange faces peering from the windows of the rectory building.

There are many ghost stories associated with the St. James-Sag grounds, many of which have been confirmed by the various priests there. Now I don't know about you, but if several priests are willing to risk their reputations and acknowledge the presence of ghostly activity at St. James-Sag, I think I'd have to believe them.

By now you know the tale of the infamous Resurrection Mary and her association with Resurrection Cemetery. You also know about the weeping woman in white who wanders the grounds of the Archer Woods Cemetery, as well as the mysterious cloaked monks of St. James-Sag Cemetery. So what is it about Archer Avenue, and the surrounding area, that makes it so haunted? Can all the unnatural activity be attributed to the close proximity of so many cemeteries or is it something else?

The stretch of road that is now Archer Avenue was once an Indian tra,il and some believe it is this association that is the true source of all the phantom activity along Archer Avenue. In fact, there are a number of roads running through Illinois and Wisconsin, such as Green Bay Road, that have been linked to strange and possibly supernatural experiences, like significant lapses in time while driving amidst thick fog in the dark. Prior to paving and modernization, many of these roads were originally used by Native Americans in their travels by horse or on foot. Native Americans, in general, maintain strong connections to nature, so it is possible that, at one time, many of them developed a heightened "sixth sense," so to speak, that enabled them to detect supernatural bridges to other worlds beyond ours. The mystical energies that would surround such places might also appeal to the many apparitions and ghosts that have been spotted in these same areas since. So perhaps it is inevitable that certain locations are marked by supernatural happenings.

Last, but not least, is the tale of the dancing devil. Years ago, in the neighborhood of Bridgeport, dances were regularly held at Kaiser Hall on Archer Avenue. During one of these dances, a lovely young lady had the pleasure of meeting a charming stranger, with good looks to boot. They were enjoying an evening of dancing and laughter when things quickly took a turn for the worse. The girl suddenly screamed in horror, quickly gaining the attention of everyone in the ballroom—many of whom knew her personally, unlike the stranger with whom she danced. Soon after, everyone's attention turned to the handsome stranger and it was assumed that he had tried to make a move on the girl. The anonymous man wisely realized the risk of sticking around and attempted to escape, but was quickly cornered by an angry mob of men. Despite being on the second floor of the building, the man jumped out a nearby window. When the other men looked out after him, they couldn't believe their eyes when he landed safely on both feet without injury. Upon closer inspection it was finally clear what had made the young girl scream. There pressed into the sidewalk where the stranger had so easily landed without incident was the distinct imprint of a hoof. And that was the night the devil came to dance along Archer Avenue.

The Legacy of Lincoln Park and the Old City Cemetery

You might be familiar with Lincoln Park and the neighboring Lincoln Park Zoo. Perhaps you've even picnicked in the park on a sunny summer afternoon. The picturesque park has been enjoyed by Chicagoans for years. But what many do not know is that the lovely Lincoln Park was once the site of Chicago's main city cemetery. When city officials decided to relocate the cemetery, so that the space could be used for something else, many of the bodies buried there were transported to either Graceland Cemetery or Rosehill Cemetery. It is quite possible that some of those who were "relocated" were less than thrilled and no longer lay at rest, as there have been hauntings in both cemeteries ever since.

Graceland Cemetery began receiving bodies from the old city cemetery in the early 1860s and boasts quite an entourage of notable Chicagoans. Among those buried there are Marshall Field, Allan Pinkerton, Louis Sullivan, Potter Palmer, and George Pullman, designer of the railroad sleeper car. Amidst the various graves in Graceland Cemetery are numerous monuments and statues paying tribute to those who rest there.

While not necessarily associated with anything supernatural, there is one particular statue that has become quite the sight to see. It is a looming eight-foot statue marking the final resting place of former hotel owner Dexter Graves. The entire statue was originally all black in color, but time and the elements have eroded and discolored it so much that it is now a much lighter green hue, exposing the bronze metal it was made from. The strange thing about the statue is that despite the worn appearance of the rest of the statue, the face remains solid black and is barely visible past the sculpted robe that partially covers it. It is truly an eerie sight. It's as if the eyes of the cloaked figure are staring into yours.

Now I'll admit that when I first examined photos of the figure, I thought it was just a joke. It looked like someone had thrown a robe over themselves and posed in an ominous position in front of a grave site for fun. There was simply something lifelike about that figure that came through even in the photos. But a visit to the cemetery will reveal this is no prank, and you'll be able to see the strange statue for yourself. Be careful if you do though. Some say you can observe your own impending death when you look into the dark face of the cloaked figure. Consequently, the figure has come to be called the "Statue of Death."

Aside from the fascinating figure with the dark face, there are actual accounts of apparitions in the cemetery. There have been many different ghost sightings in Graceland Cemetery, but the most intriguing is by far the story of little Inez Clarke.

Inez was only six years old when she died, purportedly after being struck by lightening while picnicking with her family. In memory of Inez, her parents had a life size statue sculpted in her image. The statue was placed above her grave and secured in a glass casing to keep it safe from inclement weather and vandals. Little Inez died in 1880, and the statue was placed on her grave the following year and has remained in impeccable condition all these years.

Now what is interesting about this statue is that it seems to have acquired a life of its own, and on stormy nights, when lightening is present, it disappears. Different guards patrolling the cemetery at night have walked past the grave of little Inez Clark and discovered the glass case that houses the statue to be empty. What's even more startling is that each time this has occurred, the statue is always found to be back in the glass case the very next morning. Is it possible that the spirit of Inez has merged with the life size statue replica of herself and flees in fear whenever lightening threatens to strike again? That might very well be the case as several observers have spotted a young girl dressed in clothing from an era past wandering alone in the dark cemetery with only the light of the moon to accompany her.

In addition to Graceland Cemetery being an alternate resting place for many who had previously been buried in the old city cemetery, so also was Rosehill Cemetery. And like Graceland Cemetery, Rosehill Cemetery is also the final resting place for many prominent Chicagoans, including mayors, millionaires, and local celebrities. In fact, some of these personalities might still be seeking attention from the grave. Rosehill Cemetery is home to a mausoleum that was constructed sometime during the early 1900s. The mausoleum is large enough to contain several different rooms, each one devoted to a different family. For those with the financial means and clout to secure such a room, they were given free reign over the interior design of their family's room.

Some of the more notable individuals to have been laid to rest there include John G. Shedd, former president of Marshall Field Company and benefactor of the world famous Chicago Shedd Aquarium. Also in the Rosehill Cemetery Mausoleum are Aaron Montgomery Ward and Richard Warren Sears. It should be obvious by their names that, like John Shedd, these men were also affiliated with major department store companies. In the business world, Ward and Sears were in stiff competition with one another, so to say they weren't fond of each other would be putting it lightly. Ironically, these two followed each other to the grave where they now lay within the same structure for all of eternity.

Cemetery mausoleum, much like the one that hosts Sears and Ward.
Photo courtesy of Christina Matyskela

But rumor has it that they don't necessarily lay in peace. On certain nights, a gentleman dressed in a top hat and coat tails can be seen walking about in the mausoleum. The man is always seen exiting the room belonging to the Sears family before ultimately heading in the direction of the Ward family room. So is it Sears who leaves his tomb to go have it out with Ward, or is it Ward who has been seen departing from the Sears family room on his way back to his own tomb? Most accounts suggest this supernatural figure is that of Richard Warren Sears and that his rivalry with Ward did not die with him, but instead, followed them both to the grave. Then again, maybe they both just enjoy reminiscing about the good old days.

Aside from these two business moguls, another wealthy entrepreneur with his own mausoleum is alleged to haunt the cemetery as well. Real estate tycoon Charles Hopkinson died in 1885. Construction on a cathedral-like mausoleum for Hopkinson began immediately after. But before it was complete, another family with loved ones already buried in Rosehill Cemetery contested construction of the cathedral style structure. They worried it might obstruct the view of their own family's place of burial. The case went to court and the Hopkinson family won, so construction resumed on the mausoleum. Despite finally being finished, it seems these two feuding families have eternally disturbed the spirit of Charles Hopkinson who can be heard moaning and rattling chains from inside his tomb on the anniversary of his death every year.

A female counterpart to Charles Hopkinson might also have been haunting the grounds of Rosehill Cemetery regularly were it not for her niece. On a crisp October evening in 1995, one of the cemetery's groundskeepers observed a woman standing alone near a tree in an isolated area of the cemetery. The woman was wearing a flowing gown, much like something you might bury someone in. Anyway, the ground-skeeper attempted to approach the woman so that he could escort her out of the cemetery, which was now closed for the evening. As you might have guessed, the woman disappeared before the man could reach her.

But she didn't just disappear. As the groundskeeper got closer, he realized the woman was not actually standing on the ground, but floating just above it. And as he approached her, he watched her virtually evaporate into a mist before disappearing completely.

The groundskeeper immediately recounted the occurrence to the rest of the staff in the office. The very next day, cemetery staff received an unusual request from a woman who claimed her aunt had visited her in a dream the prior night. The woman on the phone said that there was a small plot in the cemetery where several members of her family were buried. For some reason, the grave of the woman's aunt, the same aunt who appeared to her in a dream, had gone unmarked all these years. In the dream, the woman's aunt asked her to have the grave marked so that she would not be forgotten.

Later on, after taking the phone call, a few groundskeepers located the family plot the woman had described. They needed to confirm its location and determine what type of gravestone would work there. When they located the actual spot where the woman's aunt was buried, a chill surely ran down their spines when they realized it was the exact spot on which the other groundskeeper had previously seen the enigmatic woman.

Once a headstone was finally placed atop the woman's grave, she never returned. But who knows, had her niece disregarded the dream and not contacted cemetery staff, the woman might still be wandering the cemetery grounds haunting it just as Sears and Hopkinson still do.

The Miracle Child
& The Italian Bride

There are so many more cemeteries in Chicago and the surrounding suburbs that also boast hauntings of their own, but which will go unmentioned here as there are simply too many tales to tell. However, it would be remiss of me not to mention the "Miracle Child" of Holy Sepulcher Cemetery or the "Italian Bride" of Mount Carmel Cemetery. Both have come to be quite infamous among the local ghost proponents of Chicago.

Holy Sepulcher Cemetery is home to the grave of Mary Alice Quinn, although you wouldn't know it by her gravestone. Mary was a rare child who had healing hands. She apparently healed a number of ill individuals with whom she came in contact from around her neighborhood. She was a phenomenon. Even more shocking than her healing powers, though, was her sudden and untimely death at age fourteen.

Before her death, Mary had become somewhat of a celebrity because of her miraculous healing abilities. So when she died, her family feared an onslaught of graveside visitors. Rather than place her in a grave with her own headstone, the family buried Mary Alice near a marker for the Reilly family, hoping to maintain some privacy. And although Mary Alice Quinn died in 1935, an ethereal likeness of her was often observed by people the world over beginning in the late 1930s and early 1940s. Since that time, the location of her grave has become general knowledge and swarms of visitors have come to pay their respects over the years, often hoping that her healing powers will extend beyond the grave.

In some instances, it seems they have, as various people have reported recovering from serious injuries or illnesses shortly after having visited her grave. What is especially compelling about Mary's story is that sometimes the unmistakable scent of roses lingers in the air around Mary's grave, even when the cold Chicago winter has wiped out all plant life. The sweet scent of flowers where none exist has long been associated with the presence of loving spirits and can be quite comforting. Mary Alice Quinn, no doubt, wishes to extend her healing hands and her heart to all those who seek comfort from her gentle spirit. She was a "miracle child" in life, and continues to be miraculous even in death.

Unlike the inconspicuous burial of Mary Alice Quinn, the gravesite of the "Italian Bride" is marked by a life-size statue of the woman in her wedding dress. The woman was Julia Buccola Petta and she died giving birth in 1921, when she was just twenty years old. Julia was buried in Mount Carmel Cemetery, which is the same cemetery where the infamous Al Capone is also buried, among other Chicago gangsters.

Following Julia's death, her mother started experiencing some very strange dreams that would continue for more than six years. Julia's mother, Filomena, dreamt that Julia was visiting her in the dreams and begging for help because she was still alive inside that coffin. The persistence of the dreams became quite unsettling, and Filomena decided she'd better have her daughter exhumed, just in case.

No one would listen, so for six years Filomena continued to experience these extraordinarily realistic dreams before anyone would help her. Then, finally, after six plus years, Filomena was granted permission to exhume Julia's body, which she did. Much to everyone's surprise, Julia Buccola Petta lay in her coffin untouched, by anything. Her body had not yet begun to decompose, despite a time lapse of more than six years, although the casket in which she lay did show some signs of decay.

Looking at Julia in the re-opened casket, the "Italian Bride" appeared only to be sleeping. Since that time, there have been reports of a woman wearing a bridal gown wandering around the area near Julia's grave. On one occasion, she even attempted to reach out to a young boy who had gotten separated from his family while at the cemetery. When the family finally found their young son, they saw him walking hand in hand with a mysterious woman dressed in a white bridal gown. As they approached their son, the compassionate woman simply disappeared.

If all those ghostly sightings are of Julia Buccola Petta, why isn't she at rest? Maybe her mother was on to something and Julia had not actually been dead when she was first buried, but in a deep coma, in which case she would have suffocated slowly and horribly. A death like that would surely cause a spirit to become restless.

Gangster Ghosts

Chicago's rich and diverse history is not without its dark side. The city was once home to several notorious mobsters, including the infamous Al Capone and real life Robinhood John Dillinger. These two individuals were both notorious in their hey day for living on the other side of the law. Notoriety would also follow each to the grave, and beyond, as their reputations continue to precede them even in death.

But it would seem their lives of crime would not be the only thing associated with their names. For instance, some rather gruesome murders attributed to Capone are said to have produced more than a few spirits that now haunt the site where the brutal killings occurred. Capone would even be hounded by one of those ghosts during the twilight years of his life. And while Capone's spirit is not thought to be lingering anywhere, the ghost of another gangster is. The spirit of John Dillinger is sometimes seen running near Chicago's long standing Biograph Theater.

So it seems, even in death, Capone and Dillinger continue to maintain a presence in Chicago, as do the ghosts of many other slain victims who lost their lives at the hands of various criminals in and around the great city of Chicago. There are some crimes just so horrific, they scorch an indelible imprint upon the world that transcends both time and space, leaving behind something supernatural.

Capone and the
St. Valentine's Day Massacre

It is a quiet February morning. Few people are out walking in the winter weather, and so you do not encounter many faces as you continue on your way. Just as you are passing by a large warehouse, the almost eerie silence is broken by the loud hail of machine guns firing nearby. You quickly take cover in the alley, not wanting to be shot yourself. After a few minutes you hear some cars drive off. Several more minutes pass and it seems everyone has gone, so you poke your head up to have a look around.

There's no one in sight. You know you should get out of there as fast as possible, but curiosity gets the better of you. You snoop around the warehouse building and find a way in. It is noticeably warmer than the frigid winter temperature outside. Standing alone inside, an unsettling feeling soon overwhelms you. You should leave, but you don't. Instead, you walk through the desolate interior of the warehouse until you come across a scene so dreadful, you almost lose your breakfast. There in front of you, lying in a vast puddle of blood that blends with the red brick wall of the warehouse, are seven bodies. It was a bloody beginning to St. Valentine's Day, 1929.

The slaughterhouse scene just described was the work of Chicago's most infamous gangster, Alphonse Capone. He had set up some of his fellow mobsters. Seven men met up at a specified warehouse to wait for a truckload of smuggled liquor to arrive. But instead of liquor, the men would discover a surprise awaited them. They were soon joined by five other gentlemen, three of whom wore police uniforms. The seven gangsters were instructed to line up along a brick wall, after which they were blasted with a hail storm of machine gun fire. Each one dropped to the ground drenched in blood. All seven were dead. It had been a massacre. That day would go down in infamy as one of the bloodiest days in Chicago history, and would forever become known as the St. Valentine's Day Massacre. The entire thing had been arranged by Capone.

The deaths of those seven mobster men would not be the end of it all, nor would it be the end of them. The seven would return to that bloody brick wall time and again, as if permanently bound to it. After the bloody massacre that Valentine's morning, numerous reports of strange sightings at the site of the bloodbath began circulating. When passing by the once blood-spattered brick wall, you could sometimes see seven dark figures standing against it, and even hear the faint sounds of screams and machine guns. Anyone who witnessed this supernatural sighting would immediately experience an intense sense of terror. These eerie encounters would continue until the building was torn down in 1967.

But before demolition, the bricks of the wall along which the seven were slaughtered would be saved by a forward-thinking businessman who would later incorporate them into a night club he built. It made for a nice hook to draw business into the club. People were certainly intrigued, and came to the club to see Capone's wall of death. Years later after the club closed, the owner sold the bricks off individually for a grand a pop. Strangely, terrible events often befell the buyers of the bricks who began returning them to the club owner.

It seems the bricks were cursed. Many of those who had bought a brick or two suffered serious illnesses, bankruptcy, ruined relationships, and even death in some cases. The plight of the seven men who had been so brutally gunned down all those years ago would now plague anyone who came in contact with the brick remnants of that horrible history. Some people say you can still catch a glimpse of the grisly scene when visiting the location where the warehouse once stood. And for those skeptics out there, try walking a dog past the area and see if it doesn't start barking ferociously at what would seem to be nothing.

For those who would see the seven spirits lining the wall, the moment was brief. But for Capone, it would last a lifetime. Per Al Capone himself, one vengeful spirit of the seven would haunt him, following him everywhere he went, until only the sweet relief of death could save him from the madness. Although Capone evaded arrest and prosecution for the slayings, as well as virtually all his other crimes, he would eventually serve time for tax evasion. He would even serve much of his sentence at the inescapable Alcatraz.

But incarceration would not be his worst punishment. While in the slammer, Capone found himself being haunted by the ghost of one of his Valentine's Day victims. The ghost of Jimmy Clark, brother-in-law to Bugs Moran, who was another notorious mobster and also Capone's nemesis, hounded Capone so persistently that Capone started losing his grip on reality, and many of his fellow inmates thought him slowly going insane. Capone could be heard in his cell pleading with the ghost. Even after his release years later, Jimmy Clark's ghost stuck by Capone's side and refused him a moment's peace, until he died in 1947, eighteen long years after the Valentine's Day bloodfest Capone had orchestrated. If you ask me, Capone had it worse than his seven Valentine's Day victims. Their moment of hell was over in an instant, but Capone would continue to be haunted by it for life.

Dillinger's Hoax

During the era of Al Capone another infamous outlaw was also running around the streets of Chicago, seen as something of a modern day Robinhood by the public. His name was John Dillinger and he would become one of the FBI's most wanted. Dillinger was a bank robber, plain and simple. The public didn't seem to mind his misguided methods because he was stealing from the rich, an elite group with whom most people could not identify. It was the Great Depression and people everywhere were struggling and frustrated because no one would help them. So when someone like John Dillinger helped himself to some much-needed money, people could understand. Further, not only didn't they find much fault with Dillinger, the public really liked him.

Suddenly, stories started floating around that Dillinger was actually giving away a ton of the money he had stolen to struggling families who most needed it. There is no official documentation indicating whether or not Dillinger was, in fact, donating money to the poor, but his exploits would long be described in Robinhood terms. As far as the public was concerned, Dillinger was stealing from the rich in order to give to the poor. In reality, while he might have generously given a few dollars to various individuals here and there, his primary motivation in stealing was to profit for himself, and the FBI was not impressed.

In between his bank robbing escapades, like anyone else, Dillinger enjoyed an evening out on the town. Little did he know that a trip to the theater would be his last outing ever. In 1934, accompanied by two women, Dillinger headed downtown to the Biograph Theater on North Lincoln Avenue. What he didn't know sitting inside that theater was that there would soon be a far more spectacular scene happening outside its doors.

As Dillinger relaxed and watched the show, FBI agents waited patiently outside. What was even worse was that one of the women who had persuaded him to visit the theater that day was in cahoots with the FBI. She had set John Dillinger up. Police and FBI agents knew in advance that Dillinger would be at the Biograph. He didn't stand a chance. More than two hours after arriving, the show finally ended, and Dillinger exited the theater. He was only outside a moment when he came face to face with an FBI agent and realized what was about to happen.

Standing there on the sidewalk in front of the alley that ran alongside the Biograph Theater, John Dillinger was fatally shot three times by the agent. He collapsed upon the sidewalk and died there in front of the alleyway. The FBI had finally gotten their man. After the Cook County Coroner finished doing his job, Dillinger's body was temporarily placed on display for the public to see. All that separated intrigued citizens from Dillinger's body in the Cook County Morgue was a thin pane of glass. Onlookers lined up at the morgue to look through a window and take a final peak at the legendary John Dillinger.

Sometime after his death, strange events began occurring in and around the Biograph Theater. Icy cold spots were often observed even when the surrounding temperature was quite warm. Unexplained drafts sometimes wafted through. And there was a general sense of apprehension experienced by many who visited the theater or passed through the adjacent alley. But none of that compares to the most compelling evidence of the haunting that now afflicts the Biograph Theater and alleyway.

An obscure bluish apparition has been seen by many witnesses running through the alleyway next to the theater. Each time, the dark figure falls after running part way down the alley and then suddenly vanishes. This strange sighting has been observed by various individuals throughout the years, and most people choose to avoid ever taking the alleyway now, despite its convenient shortcut through to Halstead Street.

The Biograph Theater and adjoining alley are still said to be haunted even today, but there's more to the story. All these years, the ghost of gangster John Dillinger has been believed to haunt the dark alleyway next to the theater where he was brutally shot and killed. For all of Dillinger's fame and the public's fascination with him, J. Edgar Hoover's FBI had finally had the last word when they gunned him down that day. Or maybe not.

Many people would eventually question the events of that fatal day. The body that lay on display for so many people to see might not actually have been that of John Dillinger.

It would seem Dillinger had the last laugh. He might have sent his female friend to consort with the enemy, the FBI, setting them up to believe they had gotten one over on Dillinger. The entire time they waited outside for their sitting duck to emerge, they might have been waiting for the wrong guy. Dillinger and his companions might have tricked a Dillinger look-alike into going to the theater that day while the real John Dillinger made his escape out of the city. The unsuspecting doppelganger could quite possibly have been the one to take a hit that day. Many people have theorized that Dillinger fled the state and lived out his life quietly away from all the notoriety.

So whose ghost haunts the Biograph Theater and alleyway? Is it that of John Dillinger or his twin? There is really no proof one way or the other, but what is for certain is that a phantom figure wanders the alleyway, sometimes replaying the fateful events of that dark day in 1934, when police and FBI agents were operating under a "shoot to kill" policy. That would be enough to cause the spirit of any unsuspecting person to linger on after death, trying to figure out what had happened and why.

Holmes' Murder Castle

If you've ever seen any of the *Saw* movies, the movie *Hostel*, or even Rob Zombie's *House of a Thousand Corpses*, then you have some knowledge of the demented mind of a killer who gets his kicks torturing gullible victims, both physically and mentally. It's not enough to simply rape or mutilate his victims. The killer wishes to also get inside their heads, because once there, he can better understand their fears and desires. He will then use those very personal motivations to concoct an intricate and horrendous agony for each of his victims, taunting them with the fact that they will be tortured and eventually killed. The torment might continue for hours or even days, possibly longer. In those final hours, when his victims finally realize their fate, they can give up in hopelessness or they can fight to escape the madness. The torture that is inflicted upon the victims in films of this genre is often so gruesome, it's difficult to imagine it could ever be real. But what if I were to tell you it was?

Herman Webster Mudgett, otherwise known as Dr. Henry H. Holmes, is often considered one of the first American serial killers. And he didn't just kill. He constructed a "castle" full of secret torture chambers in which he is estimated to have killed as many as two hundred plus people.

It was 1893, and the Columbian Exposition World's Fair had come to Chicago, bringing with it a multitude of unsuspecting victims. There would be a long list of missing persons after the World's Fair ended. So many tourists had come to Chicago's newly constructed "White City" to enjoy the Columbian Exposition, but not all of them would leave when it was over.

Herman Mudgett was apparently unhappy with his name and decided to go by the name Henry H. Holmes. But the name change itself wasn't enough; he had to tack on the title of Dr. He passed himself off as a pharmacist. It would be several years later when the reason for his interest in drugs and chemicals would finally become obvious to everyone else.

Dr. Henry H. Holmes secured himself a position in a local drugstore in the area of Chicago now known as Englewood. The drugstore was owned by a pleasant woman, whose business was booming so much that she simply could not do it all alone. And that's where Dr. Holmes entered the picture. He was hired on to help out in the busy drugstore and spent his days mixing various medicinal concoctions for his customers. As business continued to soar, Dr. Henry Holmes found his popularity in the community also increasing, particularly among the women of the neighborhood. His charismatic personality was enticing and people seemed naturally drawn to him. Things were really going well for him, and they were about to get even better. The drugstore owner apparently decided to relocate and sold the store to Dr. Holmes, at least that's what he said.

In time, as Holmes enjoyed increasing financial success, he eventually purchased the property across the street from the drugstore. The property was empty and it was the perfect place to build a large hotel, and just in time for the arrival of the much anticipated Columbian Exposition World's Fair. The fair would surely bring in a lot of business, as all those people would need somewhere to stay. And so began construction on an enormous building that would serve as a hotel on the upper floors and as host to various storefronts street level. Once the block length building was complete, amazed neighbors dubbed it "the castle." Holmes preserved a portion of the building for his own quarters where he would live with one of his wives, as well as his mistress.

There was a seedy side to Dr. Holmes that preceded his arrival in the Windy City and that would not be revealed for several years after. Holmes had abandoned a wife and child years earlier, only to marry another woman upon arriving in Chicago. The marriage wouldn't last, though, and Holmes' second wife would leave him. He then acquired a mistress who was already married to someone else. The woman's husband left her, rightly so, and she remained in "the castle" with Holmes and her daughter for several years, even after he would become engaged to another woman. Needless to say, conflict ensued. It wouldn't last, though, as Holmes' mistress and her daughter soon went missing. Holmes was now free to pursue a life with his new fiancé Minnie.

While Holmes and Minnie lived in their castle, they hosted countless guests, most of whom were women, and many of whom would never see the light of day again. Holmes and Minnie lived something of a Bonnie and Clyde lifestyle in secret. Minnie regularly helped lure innocent victims to the castle with the promise of employment or a place to stay. Once there, these unsuspecting individuals would soon find themselves part of Holmes' many macabre experiments. Holmes and Minnie carried on this way for a while before taking their act on the road. The pair had some family business to attend to that would take them away from the castle temporarily, although that didn't mean they took a break from killing.

As they traveled the country, they killed more victims, some of whom were family members. Then, before returning to Chicago, Holmes and Minnie met a young woman named Georgianna. While on the road still, Homes and Georgianna were married with Minnie as their witness. The threesome then returned to Chicago, but Holmes' large castle was not big enough, and Minnie soon disappeared like so many others before her.

Holmes covert and deviant life persisted. He even took out life insurance policies on many of his victims before killing them. The masquerade continued for quite some time before authorities finally caught on to Holmes for insurance fraud. An investigation into Holmes' financial indiscretions would also reveal much more profound criminal exploits.

By this time, authorities were already attempting to locate swarms of people who had gone missing during the World's Fair. The missing persons cases and the insurance fraud investigation of Dr. Holmes soon overlapped, and the horrors of the "murder castle" would begin to unfold. Once investigators traced the paths of many of the missing persons to Holmes' castle, they would still not fully realize what they were dealing with. But as their investigation proceeded, they began uncovering horrors that one would have previously thought only possible in the imagination.

The "castle" soon became the "murder castle" as bodies and body parts were discovered throughout the building. Not only that, there were a series of bizarre chambers, airtight rooms, and secret passageways. Many of the rooms intended for guests had trap doors leading to smaller coffin like rooms that were actually gas chambers. The house also contained contraptions for sending bodies down chutes to the basement. In the basement, various toxic chemicals were discovered, along with an extensive collection of blood spattered surgical equipment. There was even a crematorium down there, as well as an acid vat. Holmes had constructed a regular house of horrors.

About a month after investigators had completely excavated the house and had pulled out the remains of all the victims they could find, the building mysteriously burned down. To this day, no one is sure whether a business associate of Holmes torched the macabre castle to cover up additional instances of insurance fraud, or if sickened neighbors decided to destroy the murder castle in an effort to rid their neighborhood of the ghastly evil that had been there.

The property remained empty for several years, just as it was prior to construction of the castle. But from among the ash and charred rubble, neighbors could sometimes hear unexplained moaning and anguished cries coming from the former site of the murder castle. Holmes' victims would never rest in peace after the horrendous acts he had inflicted upon them.

Eventually, a post office was built on a portion of the barren land, but the memory of what had happened there long ago was like a stain that could not be washed away. Pedestrians still noticed strange sounds and disturbances around the new post office, animals seemed to fear the place, and even postal workers reported experiencing some very chilling paranormal activity inside the building.

Holmes' life might be considered a precursor to some of the macabre movies we enjoy today, but in his case, it was all real, none of it fantasy. Authorities have never been able to determine the exact number of victims killed by Holmes. He only confessed to about twenty-seven murders, but the number of victims is believed to be significantly higher.

Among those murders he confessed to is that of the original owner of the drugstore he acquired, after telling everyone she had sold it to him before moving out of state. The mistress he had been living with when he became engaged to Minnie was also another of his victims, as was the woman's young daughter. And good old Minnie, Holmes' accomplice and confidant, was also killed by him. (She should have seen that coming.) Lucky for his first wife and child, they were left behind before Holmes constructed his crazy castle, as is true of his second wife, who had the sense to leave him when he pulled some shady attempts at forgery in an effort to swindle the woman's father. Otherwise, both women might have found themselves among his countless cast of victims.

Holmes was convicted of those twenty-seven killings to which he confessed, and was subsequently sentenced to death. While incarcerated and awaiting execution, Holmes was asked the million dollar question, "Why'd you do it?" Holmes explanation was perhaps almost more horrific than the crimes he committed.

Dr. Henry "Herbert Mudgett" Holmes callously claimed none of it was his fault. He was of the devil and was born to torture and kill. Holmes believed Satan had been with him since birth, so that it was in his nature to carry out the ghastly acts he had committed. So it would seem that the now infamous murder castle was also the devil's playground. As was appropriate, Holmes was hanged to death. Satan's spawn would hang by his neck for a full fifteen minutes before being pronounced dead, as his neck did not immediately snap upon springing the trap on which he stood. As observers watched his body hanging there, they could see it twitching involuntarily every so often. Perhaps in crossing the line from life to death, some of his victims were able to exact a bit of revenge on his dying self. For the rest, they are unfortunately bound to the gruesome site on which they were tortured and will likely haunt it for eternity.

The Chicago Sausage King and the Sausage Vat Murder

It seems Al Capone was not the only criminal to be haunted by the ghost of one of his victims. Chicago's original "Sausage King," Adolph Luetgert, would find himself in a similar predicament later in life, whereby his ghost would follow him to his grave.

Luetgert was a German immigrant who came to Chicago sometime during the 1870s to sell sausages. He was a hit and business flourished, so much so that he decided to have his own factory built. A huge meat packing plant was constructed at the corner of Hermitage and Diversey in 1894, and the legend of the Sausage King was born. Luetgert even had a charming three-story house built for himself next to the factory.

The Sausage King had everything going for him, a beautiful home, a thriving business, and an active social life. All he needed was a wife, which he would soon find. While out and about one day, the popular Sausage King would meet a pretty petite young woman named Louisa, who was practically half his size. Luetgert was quickly quite enthralled with her and began wooing her. Louisa was from a rather meager background by comparison, but soon found herself immersed in a world of lavish gifts and exciting evenings out. She, too, quickly became enchanted with Chicago's Sausage King and the pair was married. As a token of his love and adoration, the Sausage King gave his bride a gorgeous gold ring inscribed with her new initials, "L. L.," for Louisa Luetgert. Louisa wore the ring with pride.

Life was moving along for Luetgert and Louisa. They were enjoying life in their beautiful three-story home next to the sausage factory that had made it all possible. But it would not last. The mismatched couple would soon take up quarreling as a popular pastime. Their neighbors grew accustomed to the loud arguments that were easily overheard in the Luetgert home, occurring quite regularly. As their love dissipated and the marriage began to crumble, Luetgert, the Sausage King, would opt to relocate to a small room inside his grand sausage packing plant, rather than cohabitate with his estranged wife.

Not long after he began sleeping in the factory away from his wife, he found a new girlfriend. He really didn't have to look too far to find her. He began dating one of the servant women who worked in the large three-story home next door where his wife still lived. His new girlfriend also happened to be his wife's niece. That news couldn't have come easily to Louisa. So what's a woman to do when her husband has left her to take up residence in his sausage factory with his wife's own niece, a girl who had previously been living with the both of them? A woman in Louisa's position might have considered killing her cheating husband. It happens all the time. But Louisa would not harm her husband. It would be the other way around.

Louisa turned up missing one day, and her two boys began to wonder what happened to her. Their Sausage King father brushed off their concerns and simply said that she had gone to stay with their aunt. When Louisa did not return several days later, the boys' uncle, Louisa's brother, reported her missing to the police and an investigation ensued. It turns out that on the night Louisa went missing, she was seen with her husband in the sausage factory. At least two plant employees claimed to have seen the quarreling pair together that night. And one of those employees was told by Luetgert to take the rest of the evening off. He thought nothing of it and went on his way. That was the last time anyone would see Louisa Luetgert alive. After that evening, she disappeared and was never seen again, at least not in her earthly state.

Luetgert claimed his wife had left of her own accord and had decided not to return. Police believed something more sinister had happened. As they began investigating, they grew increasingly suspicious of Luetgert, until he was finally charged with Louisa's murder. The Sausage King swore himself innocent, though. But mounting evidence suggested otherwise. Remember that stunning gold ring engraved with the initials L.L.? Detectives discovered that ring in one of the sausage vats along with a tiny fragment of bone. After Luetgert's indictment, despite the lack of a body or any witnesses, he was tried and found guilty of the murder of his wife Louisa Luetgert.

Many Chicagoans speculated that the Sausage King had ground his wife's body up with the sausage meat. Consequently, many former customers stopped purchasing the King's sausages. The police had a different explanation. They believed Luetgert had boiled Louisa's body in acid and then burned the remains in a furnace inside the sausage packing plant. Several chemicals had been discovered there during the investigation and it seemed a likely explanation of Louisa Luetgert's final fate.

Soon after his conviction, the Sausage King became acquainted with his new home in the Joliet State Prison. While incarcerated, the once successful Sausage King began to come undone. Prison guards often heard him talking to himself. When confronted, he always gave the same response. His dead wife was haunting him as revenge for her death.

Interesting he would say that, considering he never acknowledged her death and insisted she was only missing. Further, he always maintained his innocence. It was quite clear he was being haunted not only by his murdered wife, but also by his own guilt over what he had done. Louisa Luetgert's ghost would continue to haunt the Sausage King throughout his entire stay in Joliet, and would even follow him until his own death in 1900.

It seems she took a break from haunting him on occasion, though, as many of the neighbors who used to overhear her fighting with Luetgert when they still lived together, witnessed her spirit in the house numerous times. They reported seeing

Louisa Luetgert dressed in white standing near the fireplace in her home. Others observed her wandering around inside the sausage factory next door. The house had a number of occupants who rented rooms there after Louisa was killed and Luetgert was sitting in prison for her murder. Most of these folks didn't stick around for very long. It seems they weren't comfortable sharing the house with Louisa's ghost.

In recent years, the neighborhood once ruled by the great Sausage King, has had a face lift. The grand old houses of yesteryear have since been replaced by modern homes, and the infamous sausage factory has been converted to condominiums. The place would be virtually unrecognizable to Luetgert and Louisa these days, but she is still said to roam her old neighborhood on the anniversary of her death every year. It seems Louisa's untimely demise has left her spirit restless, but there is no question as to whose fault that was. The Sausage King was guilty as charged. So the only question to still remain is whether she had, in fact, been ground into sausage meat and distributed around the unsuspecting city.

Robinson Woods and the Schuessler-Peterson Murders

Have you ever thought the woods were a creepy place to be? If you watch any number of horror movies, you'll witness various atrocities occurring almost always in a wooded setting. The woods seem to be a natural source of terror for many and serve as a secluded spot for supernatural activities to go relatively unnoticed. We've already explored the wooded area of Bachelor's Grove Cemetery that is ripe with all sorts of spirits. And so too are the old Indian burial grounds within Robinson Woods just off Lawrence Avenue and not far from Chicago's O'Hare Airport, which has its own host of hauntings.

If you dare set foot inside Robinson Woods, you are likely to observe some unusual activity. Many witnesses have reported seeing ghostly figures dressed in Native American garb and hearing the sound of a slow and steady drum beat wafting through the woods. Some people have even detected the scent of flowers when none are around, particularly in the cold winter months. According to ghost researcher Dale Kaczmarek and author Troy Taylor, some of the tribal drum sounds reportedly heard by witnesses in the woods have actually been recorded on tape. No explanation has ever been obtained for the strange tribal sounds on the tape and they are believed to be of supernatural origin.

Robinson Woods once belonged to the Andrew Robinson family who, for years, resided there in their home before it burned down in 1955. Although the family relocated after losing their house, upon death, many of them were buried in the woods they once called home. There is now only a single stone marking the site of the Robinson family graves. Andrew Robinson was one half Native American on his mother's side and remained involved in tribal activities throughout his life, hence the association between Robinson Woods, Indian burial grounds, and tribal drum sounds.

Documentation of supernatural activity in these woods has persisted over the years, but not all of it can be attributed to sacred Indian rituals or the Robinson family. In the same year the Robinson home burned down, the bodies of three young boys were also discovered in Robinson Woods. Many people believe the spirits of those innocent youngsters have been haunting Robinson Woods ever since.

The scene was truly horrific. The bodies of Bobby Peterson and brothers, John and Anton Schuessler, were discovered bound and naked with their eyes taped closed in Robinson Woods on a crisp Autumn day in October of 1955. All three boys had died from asphyxiation. It was a gruesome crime, three young boys so harshly murdered and then discarded in the woods. It was the worst crime Chicago had seen in a long time. Detectives were stumped as to who could have killed the boys. No substantial evidence was ever found, not even the clothing of any of the three boys. The case would remain unsolved for a full forty years.

At one point, the investigation took an interesting turn when a detective on the case speculated that the boys had rendezvoused at a downtown building briefly where they met up with John Wayne Gacy, who is now perhaps considered to be the most infamous serial killer ever to come out of Chicago. Of course, at the time, John Wayne Gacy was only a teen and had not yet become the hideous monster who would molest and kill dozens of young males before stashing their remains in the crevices of his basement. Coincidentally, John Wayne Gacy happened to live only a few blocks from John and Anton Schuessler's house at the time, but it was never really known whether they had been acquainted. The detective first made the connection between Gacy and the three murdered boys when they were reportedly seen hanging around the Garland Building on the day of their disappearance, a place frequented by Gacy, that happened to be a local hot spot for gay men to meet up with one another. Researcher and author Richard Linberg first disclosed this revelation about a possible connection between John Wayne Gacy and the missing boys. But a brief five to ten minute interval when all four males might have simultaneously been in the lobby of the downtown Garland building was all there was to the story, and Gacy would have no further involvement in the case.

Forty years would pass before the murders of John and Anton Schuessler and Bobby Peterson would be solved. Were it not for an informant revealing the identity of the boys' killer, the case might never have been solved. But in 1995, there was such an informant who had been speaking to police about another case, that of a missing heiress to the Brach's candy company. For one reason or another, the gentleman ended up implicating another man in the case of the Schuessler-Peterson murders that had occurred forty years prior. The information provided by this informant would lead to the arrest and conviction of the boys' seditious killer, and the families of the two boys would finally have closure.

So what exactly happened to the Schuessler brothers and Peterson boy? On the day they disappeared, the three boys had traveled downtown to the Chicago Loop where they intended to see a movie. Later, after leaving the theater, they briefly stopped inside the Garland building lobby, where they may or may not have chatted with John Wayne Gacy. From there, the boys headed over to a nearby bowling alley where they hung out for a while, before departing for yet another bowling alley. It is believed that the three boys tried hitching a ride shortly after leaving the last bowling alley, a ride that would perhaps seal their fates. According to the police informant who had spilled the beans about a possible suspect in the murders, the killer had actually bragged to several people about the crime. The guilty party worked in the stables of a horse breeding operation at the time and convinced the three boys to accompany him there to check out the horses. Once there, he would molest and kill all three boys, one at a time. The bodies of the three boys were subsequently ditched in Robinson Woods, close to where the Des Plaines River runs through. The horse stables were then burned down to eliminate any evidence, purportedly by the owner of the stables. Prior to being arrested for the Schuessler-Peterson murders, the accused allegedly coerced other young males into participating in bizarre sexual encounters by threatening they might end up like the Schuessler brothers or Bobby Peterson if they didn't cooperate.

Even with only circumstantial evidence, the case was a slam dunk, and forty years after the horrific murders of John and Anton Schuessler and Bobby Peterson, the killer would finally be brought to justice. It's been well over fifty years since the murders took place, but if you walk through Robinson Woods over to the place where the boys' bodies were dumped, you can be sure you'll sense a strange and eerie presence, a quiet unrest.

John Wayne Gacy: The Killer Clown

John Wayne Gacy is one of the most notorious and well known serial killers of all time, and he was spawned in the city of Chicago. Most true crime buffs are likely familiar with the case of John Wayne Gacy and the gruesome nature of his crimes, that included sodomy, rape, and murder. But there's more to the story than just a friendly man who sometimes dressed up like a clown for children's parties, as he was secretly luring unsuspecting males to his home where he would sexually molest and kill them. What is unknown to many people, even to those most familiar with Gacy's crimes, is that there was something of a supernatural aftermath to his grisly deeds.

Over the course of about six years, Gacy raped and killed at least thirty-three young men. He would be convicted of all thirty-three murders. At the time, no one else in the entire country had ever been convicted of so many homicides. But before Gacy could be charged with all those crimes, evidence had to be gathered. Detectives had the daunting task of excavating Gacy's property. They found bodies in the basement in the tiniest of spaces. They found bodies buried under the garage, and they even discovered a body cemented into the back patio. Gacy had stashed bodies everywhere imaginable. He even kept the corpses of a few victims under his bed for several days before deciding on where to bury the bodies. His was truly a house of horrors.

After Gacy's property had been thoroughly searched, and he had been convicted and locked up, the decision was made to tear down the home of John Wayne Gacy. The house, the garage, and everything else on the property was demolished, including the driveway. After removing the ruins from the property, the land was completely gone over with a backhoe to ensure no bodies remained.

For a long time, the lot that once held the home of the friendly neighborhood clown, otherwise known as John Wayne Gacy, stood barren and vacant. No one wanted to build on the tainted land. Nature even seemed to shun the place. Some grass and weeds grew up around the perimeter of the property, but the soil where the house and garage once stood remained lifeless. No grass or other plant life would grow there. People began to wonder if the property wasn't cursed by the souls of Gacy's victims. Some people even thought they heard bizarre cries coming from the house before it was torn down. For years, the land remained that way, haunted by the memory of a macabre and sinister time when a clown would become a killer more than thirty times over. The cursed property could only be cured with new life.

After another home was built there and a new family moved in, things finally quieted down and the grass began to grow again. The souls of Gacy's victims might finally be at rest, but you have to wonder if he's been so lucky. Gacy was executed by lethal injection in 1994, but one never knows if he's not cursed with wandering and haunting the earth endlessly for all his transgressions.

The Gruesome Grimes Sisters Double Murder

There is a long lonely stretch of road that is marked by an unmistakable eeriness. Much like Archer Avenue, home to Resurrection Mary, German Church Road is thought to be haunted as well, but for very different reasons. Chicago author Troy Taylor has dubbed these desolate but spooky stretches of road "haunted highways." The haunted highway that is German Church Road is usually barren and does not necessarily see much traffic. However, despite the lack of travelers, there exists an obvious presence there.

A stream of water, aptly named "Devil's Creek," runs along one side of German Church Road. The area is entirely surrounded by woods. If you look closely through the trees, not far from the stream, you'll see a vacant driveway, perhaps noticeable only by the old chain that bars entrance to it. Walk a little further down the abandoned tree lined driveway, and you'll encounter the ruins of an old house that once stood there isolated in the woods. Stay a while and you will likely hear a phantom vehicle pull into the driveway and up to the place where the house used to be. With the vehicle still running, the car door opens, and moments later a loud thud can be heard as something is dumped along the side of German Church Road. You can then hear the car door slam shut, followed by the sound of the car speeding off. All the while you'll never actually see the car you can so distinctly hear.

But on some nights, it might be possible to catch a glimpse of this phantom car racing past the house, after hearing the sound of bodies being dumped. And on rare occasions, you might even witness the abandoned naked bodies of two young ladies callously left along the side of the road just above Devil's Creek. So what could have happened here to leave this place haunted by the memory of something apparently quite sinister?

As it turns out, the bodies of two teen sisters had been dumped on the other side of a guard rail running along German Church Road. The guard rail was there to prevent passing cars from plunging into the creek below, were they ever to lose control of their vehicles. The naked corpses were discovered by a passing construction worker. Once police were on the scene they realized the bodies belonged to two girls who had been missing for almost a month. The girls were Barbara and Patricia Grimes. They went missing just a few days after Christmas in 1956. The bodies showed visible bruising and puncture wounds. They had clearly been assaulted, and investigators found themselves facing a brutal crime that would continue to baffle them for decades. Whatever happened, must have been horrific because the occupants of the nearby house quickly departed after the girls' bodies were found only a short distance away, and all that remains of the house now is the driveway.

Barbara and Patricia Grimes had gone out to the movies on the evening of December 28, 1956; at least that's what they told their mom. The girls were in their teens and had been out alone before, so their mother thought nothing of it. According to their mother, the sisters planned to see a showing of *Love Me Tender,* as they were avid Elvis fans. The girls would never return home, though.

Police and concerned citizens searched for the girls over the ensuing weeks. Many people even reported seeing the girls around town on various days during the first week they went missing. Detectives were never able to confirm any of the sightings, however. Some skeptics began speculating that the girls had probably run away from home.

Of course, the family would not believe it. They were sure something or someone had prevented them from returning home after the movie that cold December night, and they held out hope the girls would be brought safely home. But all hope was shattered when the unclothed corpses of the two sisters were discovered along German Church Road on January 22, 1957.

An investigation into the deaths of the two Grimes girls produced little information and inconclusive autopsy reports didn't help things any. The coroner determined the cause of death for both girls to be shock and exposure. However, both bodies displayed noticeable injuries. Barbara Grimes, the older of the two sisters, had clear bruising on her face and head, as well as puncture wounds in her chest. Her younger sister Patricia also showed bruising to the face and had severe injuries on the abdominal area. Later accounts would even suggest sexual assault, but that was never confirmed.

Discouraged detectives seemed to be coming up with more questions than answers. They interrogated countless suspects and even elicited a confession from one, but were still unable to accurately identify the perpetrator. The confession came from a seventeen year old male who had illegally been given a polygraph test. While hooked to the polygraph equipment, the young man admitted having abducted the two sisters, but the confession could not be used because he was a minor, and it was not permissible to polygraph test anyone under the age of eighteen at the time. Ironically, that same young man would later be convicted and imprisoned for killing another young woman.

Prior to that young man's possibly coerced confession, another man had temporarily been a suspect in the brutal slayings of the Grimes sisters. The man had anonymously called the police to report a "vision" he'd had of the dead girls lying in a park around 81st Street and Wolf Road. Police were, of course, able to trace the call and were eventually able to discover the identity of the anonymous caller.

A week after the man had recounted his strange dream to police, the bodies of Barbara and Patricia Grimes were discovered along German Church Road, approximately one mile from the park located at 81st and Wolf; the same park the man had dreamed the girls' bodies were in. Naturally, he became an obvious suspect. But after being thoroughly questioned by detectives, it was clear this man was not the offender they were looking for and they were back to square one. That was until they came across a more promising suspect.

An out-of-town drifter had been spotted with the two sisters about two days after they were first reported missing. It was extremely early in the morning, so there weren't many people up yet who might have seen them. A diner owner was convinced she'd seen the two sisters in the diner accompanied by two men early one morning. She thought one of the girls seemed intoxicated at the time. One of the men, the drifter, was questioned by police several times and even taken into custody, but was eventually released without being charged. Interestingly, shortly after his release from police custody, it was discovered that there had been an outstanding warrant for his arrest in connection with the abduction and sexual assault of a thirteen year old girl. The young girl would thankfully survive the nightmare and identified the man as her assailant, only he would never be convicted of the crime. The details of the young girl's attack were strikingly similar to those surrounding the Grimes sisters' murder case, which was also beginning to remind investigators of the horrible Schuessler-Peterson murders that had occurred just one year earlier.

Like the Schuessler-Peterson case, the clothing of the Grimes Sisters would never be found. In either instance, the drifter was the most likely suspect, but since he was never charged in the Grimes' case and eluded conviction in the other, he would ultimately escape scot-free. Whoever was responsible for the gruesome deaths of the Grimes sisters would leave an indelible mark upon the lonely stretch of German Church Road that runs congruent with Devil's Creek. The events of the crime must have been so heinous that the entire area from the roadway to the creek, as well as the woods and the secluded house now marked only by a lone driveway, has all become haunted. If you think you can stomach the sickening thud of the bodies of two innocent girls snuffed out in their prime being pitched over the guard rail above Devil's Creek, you might try visiting this unholy site.

A peculiar tidbit about the area on German Church Road where the girls were found connects this place and its ghosts to some of the ghosts we were introduced to earlier along Archer Avenue. The Grimes sisters were said to sometimes visit a local establishment on Archer Avenue, the same long roadway bordered by three cemeteries, including Resurrection Cemetery. The spot where the Grimes sisters' bodies were found is actually located in the Willow Springs suburb. This entire area seems to be infested with supernatural activity, from the Willowbrook Ballroom to Resurrection Cemetery, to Monk's Castle, and Archer Woods. It is certainly a ghost hunter's paradise. But be careful. You wouldn't want to become the next ghost story yourself.

The Wynekoop Mansion

The Wynekoop Mansion, otherwise known as the "House of Weird Death," once stood grand and proud on the city's west side. From all appearances, the house was like any of the other exquisite mansions on the block. But inside the home things were not so lovely. Between an operating table in the basement, a classic case of Freud's Oedipal Complex between mother and son, an attempted strangling, and an actual murder, the House of Weird Death was certainly weird, to say the least.

It seems the house was cursed since its inception in 1901. The house was built for the Wynekoop family, which consisted of Frank and Alice Wynekoop, and their four children; Marie Louise, Earle, Walker, and Catherine. The house would also later be occupied by extended family members, as well as paying tenants, all of whom would eventually be involved in one way or another in the bizarre and twisted events that would occur in that house.

Early misfortunes in the home were ultimately attributed to a curse, although something more menacing would seem to pervade the home. Early on, one of the Wynekoop daughters, Marie Louise, fell gravely ill and died in the house. Her death was blamed on the curse. Later, Mr. Wynekoop's own brother would commit an outrageous act that would also be blamed on the mansion's curse. During the course of a bitter divorce, Frank Wynekoop's brother, Gilbert, would lose his temper and try to choke to death his soon to be ex-wife inside the Wynekoop mansion. Luckily for her he failed, but that didn't stop him from going insane over it later on. He would ultimately have to be institutionalized. Again, it had to be the curse.

By this time, the neighbors were really talking. A young daughter dies before her time and an insane sibling attempts murder. There was obviously a curse. The death of yet another family member would do nothing to dispel suspicions of a curse. The daughter-in-law of Frank and Alice Wynekoop, Rheta Wynekoop, was found dead in the home in 1933. The events surrounding her death would reveal even more troubling activities within the home, further fueling rumors of a curse.

Rheta Wynekoop was married to Earle, the dashing son of Frank and Alice Wynekoop. Earle had quite a reputation among the ladies. He was a smooth operator who managed to charm one woman after another, often promising to some day fulfill their dreams of marriage and children in order seduce them into bed. The only problem was that he was already married. Earle and his wife, Rheta, lived with his parents in their mansion. Earle regularly left Rheta alone there while he jaunted off to meet his next conquest.

Rheta became depressed with nothing to console her but her music. She was a talented violinist and had nothing but time to practice her craft, while Earle played the field. Earle's family was either oblivious to or in denial over his philandering ways, particularly his mother, Alice. Alice Wynekoop was a doctor and she adored Earle immensely. She was also a well respected member of the community who performed many charitable works. She was a model citizen, at least on the surface. Everything seemed to be in order until her daughter-in-law was found dead on an operating table in the basement of their large home.

The subsequent police investigation following Rheta's death would uncover some bizarre living arrangements in the Wynekoop mansion. In addition to the Wynekoop family and several extended family members, an old school teacher lived there as well. The home's occupants shared an intense loyalty to one another that posed quite a challenge to investigating officers attempting to solve the mystery of Rheta's murder. She had been drugged with chloroform and shot in the back just below the left shoulder blade. Depending on the angle of entry, the bullet could have possibly passed through her heart. It was the only gunshot wound reported on the body but the gun that lay next to her cold corpse had been fired three times.

The scene was surely strange, not the least of which was an operating table in the house, but Alice Wynekoop was a doctor after all, and retained the table purportedly for emergency purposes. As the investigation unfolded, Dr. Alice Wynekoop became increasingly suspicious to police. She was eventually arrested and charged with the murder of Rheta Wynekoop. Alice Wynekoop maintained her innocence while offering various excuses and explanations as to who killed Rheta. Nothing fit, however, and police continued to pressure Dr. Wynekoop.

They finally came up with a plan and concocted a story about Earle having taken out a life insurance plan on his wife just prior to her death. To her horror, Alice was told that her precious son Earle was now a primary suspect. Alice quickly concocted a story of her own to protect her son. She confessed to accidentally killing Rheta through an overdose of chloroform prior to performing a necessary, but un-named, medical procedure. Dr. Wynekoop then claimed she feared her professional reputation would be ruined over the botched procedure so she shot the already deceased Rheta to make it look like something else had happened. That's when Alice Wynekoop came up with an unlikely story about thieves breaking into her home on several occasions to steal several pharmaceutical drugs from her medical supply. The drug thieves had probably shot Rheta when she caught them stealing from Dr. Wynekoop's home office.

Detectives were not completely satisfied with Dr. Wynekoop's explanation of events. They suspected Alice's son, Earle, had masterminded the murder and that she had fabricated the entire drug stealing story to cover for him. In her eyes, Earle could do no wrong.

The unnatural attachment between mother and son brought Earle home to Chicago after having, supposedly, been away in New Mexico on business. Earle couldn't stand to have his mother in her current predicament, so he confessed to killing his own wife. Detectives were now left with two different confessions from two different suspects, each exonerating the other. The mother-son duo was given multiple lie detector tests and Earle failed each one. However, the district attorney (D. A.) was intent on prosecuting his beloved mother, so she went on trial. The D. A. claimed Alice blamed Rheta for making Earle so unhappy. Well how unhappy could the guy have been running around with all those girlfriends?

It seemed unlikely, but Dr. Wynekoop was tried for murder and found guilty. Throughout the investigation, interrogation, and subsequent trial, Earle and his mother exchanged letters back and forth. The content of those letters was apparently quite shocking. It seems the two had a much deeper connection to one another than just that of mother and son. There was some romantic love between the two quite reminiscent of Sigmund Freud's infamous Oedipus Complex that was evident in Shakespeare's *Hamlet*. So it seems the unexplained death of Rheta Wynekoop was not the only "weird" thing in that house. An unholy relationship between mother and son would be the clincher.

Ironically, while his mother was on trial for murder and he was free to run about as he had always done, Earle ended up killing someone, although unintentionally. He hit a young boy with his car and the child died. No one talked much of Earle, though. It was far more interesting to gossip about the once respected and reputable Dr. Wynekoop, who had lost her mind and murdered her own daughter-in-law.

Many believe Rheta haunted the Wynekoop Mansion after her senseless slaughter. For a while, she could sometimes be heard playing the violin. It's hard to say if she still haunts, as the Wynekoop Mansion exists no more. For that matter, most of the large homes in the neighborhood have crumbled, and only vacant plots of land remain. The area has certainly changed since the days of the rich Wynekoops and their neighbors. It is now a crime-infested area, and there are no grand mansions to be seen. But despite the absence of the original Wynekoop home, some still report hearing the soft sounds of the violin as Rheta plays on at the site of the crumbled Wynekoop estate.

Spooky Suburbs

In addition to the many haunted sites in and around the city of Chicago, including a number of cemeteries exhibiting supernatural phenomenon, many of the outlying suburbs contain their own haunted hot spots as well. Yes, the suburbs are spooky too. The entire area might just be predisposed to supernatural energies, as was known by Native American tribes so many years ago. There are hauntings in many of the large flourishing suburban areas, as well as in the smaller, more secluded rural areas. Chicago is quite the haunted metropolis, but as you venture out beyond the boundaries of the city you'll find you cannot so easily elude the pervasive supernatural manifestations that are seemingly everywhere.

Cuba Road

What do a silo, a cemetery, and an SUV all have in common? The answer is Cuba Road, a long dark stretch of roadway running through the Chicago suburb of Barrington. Cuba Road has become quite infamous among locals over the years, as unexplained events continue to occur there on a regular basis. Just driving down Cuba Road can be spooky. It is lined by trees for miles and there are very few lights along the way.

Driving down Cuba Road at night, it's easy to feel like you're lost in the middle of nowhere.

Perhaps, the most widely shared story about this desolate stretch of road is that of the small cemetery that sits along Cuba Road known as White Cemetery. The cemetery itself is extremely small, comparable to someone's backyard, but the odd events that occur there are perhaps larger than life. If you drive by the old cemetery at night you can sometimes see strange balls of light almost dancing along the fence that surrounds the small cemetery. These floating orbs of light seem to follow cars, almost teasing them, as they drive past.

So far as anyone knows, these orbs are harmless, but the large black SUV-type vehicle that is sometimes seen around White Cemetery might not be. There have been countless reports of an unidentified black vehicle leaving from the entrance to White Cemetery, and suddenly disappearing down Cuba Road after only a short distance. If you're lucky, the large vehicle will simply pass by without incident. Other times, the vehicle might closely follow you and even chase you until you run right off the road.

As for the phantom black vehicle, it always seems to disappear unscathed into the darkness of the night. No one knows who the vehicle belongs to or why it chases spectators off the road, but it seems to be a good bet someone or something doesn't like trespassers snooping around the cemetery after dark. Perhaps the floating orbs enjoy playing a sort of tug-o-war game with the black car, and you're in the middle being pulled on both ends. The dancing orbs attract your attention, luring you toward the cemetery, only to have the dark vehicle tugging at the other end attempting to force you out.

Further along Cuba Road, you'll find a peculiar house. The house is best seen under the light of a full moon with no other lights to distract from it. In other words, it's best to turn off your car's headlights, if you really want to witness this phantom house. Some nights, the house is easily noticeable due to a fiery blaze. On other nights, you can even see an old woman walking along the path leading to the house, lantern in hand. But should you try to approach the old woman or walk down the path to the house, all will be gone. The house seems to have a habit of disappearing just as suddenly as it appears. Some even believe that if you do successfully reach the house, you'd better not stick around. Legend has it that you just might disappear with the house and be lost forever.

So what's with this vanishing house? It is believed to be the spirit of a house that burned down sometime during the 1920s, which might explain the blazing fire that is sometimes spotted near it.

White Cemetery is not the only supernatural story surrounding Cuba Road. Another interesting tale concerns a child spirit who can be heard playing on a set of swings out near an old barn. The girl is sometimes heard crying, and other times laughing. Not much is known about the young girl, as most people have never actually seen her, but if you listen closely, her soft voice can be heard behind the barn. Also associated with the girl is a phantom white horse that is sometimes seen standing in front of that same barn. To find the barn, it is necessary to turn off Cuba Road onto Ela Road, an even darker and more heavily tree lined road than Cuba. If you choose to go creeping around there at night without your headlights on, please be careful. You wouldn't want to run over the ghostly girl and her toys, as was almost the case

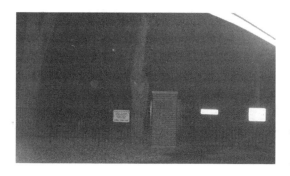

Cuba Road's White Cemetery at night with orbs of light and a peculiar tree. *Photo author's own*

when a gentleman named David took a drive through there one strange night.

David was driving along Cuba Road with a few friends. It was quite late, and so far nothing too extraordinary had happened, so they decided to take their chances down one of the side roads. They turned off Cuba Road, down a smaller one, and as they continued down the dark desolate road, things began to get spooky. It seemed to be darker the further they drove, almost as if the trees lining both sides of the road were closing in on them. But this did not deter them, and they even ventured outside the car to take a look around. Once back inside the car they continued driving further down the road until it got even darker and they were unable to see an end to the road anytime soon.

Since David was driving, he opted to turn around and head back the way they came. The narrow tree-lined road did not offer much room for maneuvering so David drove a little further until he saw what looked to be a driveway poking out from the trees. It was difficult to tell, though, since there were no lights anywhere, save for his car's. He pulled the car into the driveway and prepared to back out when he noticed a child's wagon sitting in the driveway near the rear of his vehicle. It seemed strange he hadn't seen it when he first pulled in, but didn't think much of it, until he also heard a child's soft laughter. Everyone else in the car heard it too, but there was no one else around. And what child, other than a spirit child, would be pulling a wagon around in the dark at such a late hour? Needless to say, David high tailed it out of there and did not look back.

Now about that spooky silo you were teased with earlier. The old silo does not stand on Cuba Road, but it is located in Barrington on Shoe Factory Road. There are several stories surrounding this haunted silo, and which version is the correct one is unknown. The story I always heard growing up was that a man had been hanged inside the silo for reasons that elude me now. The silo used to sit at the end of a tree-

Haunted Silo in Barrington. *Photo author's own*

lined gravel road and, as a curious teen, friends and I often drove to the silo with the intention of looking inside to get a glimpse of the macabre blood-stained interior, and perhaps feel the presence of the hanged man's spirit. We were always too chicken, though, and rarely ventured far from the car. We were never able to confirm what ghastly acts really occurred inside that silo.

Other accounts of the silo center on the nearby accompanying farm house. It is believed that, years ago, a farmer discovered his wife had been cheating on him with another man. In his rage, he went mad and killed her and their children, burying them all before also killing himself. It is said that if you stand near the spot where he buried his family, you'll observe a set of five trees, each one dead. Take a closer look and you'll realize that the trees form a five point star with each tree dotting a point on the star. It is certainly a strange sight.

Other odd occurrences have been observed in and around the house, including the silo. It seems the entire grounds are haunted by the restless spirits of the jealous farmer and his family. The tale I'd been told as a teen is quite possibly the disturbing finale to this family's gruesome story. After slaughtering the entire family inside their own home, and realizing what he had done, the farmer likely hanged himself in the silo, although some believe it may have been his wife who was hanged by the farmer in the silo.

Years after the horrific happenings of that place had long since passed, another family purchased the property and moved in. They soon began experiencing strange things like unexplained noises and an eerie presence in the house. When they finally heard about the house's heinous history, they wisely evacuated and even insisted the house be burned to the ground. Unfortunately, such efforts are usually in vain. A building can be burned to the ground, but the evil that occurred there cannot necessarily be scorched from the memory of that place, as such unspeakable acts tend to transcend time and the spirits remain restless.

Creepy Theaters

The Opera House in Woodstock is home to a ghost and her name is Elvira. Elvira has haunted the Opera House for such a long time she even has her own seat in the balcony, DD113. The seat is forever left empty for her, and it's always easy to tell when she's sitting in it because the seat will be down. Like many theaters, all the seats in the building are spring loaded, the seat in an upright position folded against the back of the chair when no one is sitting there, so that patrons can easily walk through the row to get to their own seat. But before you think a prankster is playing tricks, a set designer was working alone in the theater one evening, when he heard a noise in the direction of seat 113. He glanced upward and saw that several of the seats in that area, including 113, were all in the down position. As he walked over to investigate, the seats returned to the standard upright position. It seems Elvira might have been sitting with some spirit friends.

Elvira doesn't always take a seat though. She is sometimes known to move props and topple over scenery. She can even be heard letting out a huge sigh of disappointment from seat 113 when actors botch their lines. No one really knows who Elvira may have been. Was she an actress, a stagehand, or simply a theater patron? The details are hazy, but one possibility is that whoever she was, she might have fallen from atop a high staircase. Many actresses trying out for parts have been observed to shift into a hypnotic trance and then proceed to climb a dangerous staircase leading to some openings from which they could easily fall. Luckily, the young women are always pulled from danger and subsequently snap out of the strange trance. Is Elvira attempting to lure these young ladies to the same demise she herself suffered?

Whatever Elvira's story is, she has been described as a gorgeous woman with long blond locks and a petite figure who is usually wearing a flowing gown. She has roamed the

Opera House for several decades and isn't expected to depart anytime soon, so the next time you attend a performance at the Woodstock Opera House, be sure to take note of seat DD113. If Elvira's sitting there, perhaps you'll want to introduce yourself.

The old movie theater in Antioch is also rumored to be haunted. Theater employees and guests have observed strange noises and other phenomena on various occasions over the years. Footsteps are sometimes heard traipsing up and down the stairs when no one is there. Flood lights flash on, out of nowhere, and then turn off just as suddenly.

The spirit of a young girl who hung herself from the theater's balcony years ago is also believed to haunt the place. And perhaps the most interesting detail about the Antioch Theater is that there are purportedly secret tunnels and passageways running beneath the theater toward neighboring towns. The tunnels are believed to have been constructed by the infamous Al Capone and were possibly intended as escape routes, should he have needed to flee the police and his enemies alike while watching a flick. Too bad the Biograph Theater didn't have the same hidden feature through which John Dillinger or his doppelganger could have escaped.

The Strange Stickney Mansion

What would you call a house without any square corners inside or out? That would be the Stickney Mansion of Bull Valley in the northwest suburbs. The Stickney Mansion is now occupied by both the police department and the village hall of Bull Valley, but was originally built for the Stickney family sometime during the mid 1800s. The Stickneys were strong spiritualists and believed whole heartedly in the power of séances to summon the dead. Mr. George and Sylvia Stickney considered themselves mediums and desired a spacious home in a quiet setting where they could conduct séances regularly. Part of their motivation was to be able to contact their many deceased children. They found the perfect spot in what is now Bull Valley, and made plans to have a house built. The one critical requirement was that the house be rounded with no ninety degree corners. The Stickneys believed bad spirits liked to hide in dark corners. They didn't want to risk inviting any evil spirits when summoning good ones during séances so there could be absolutely no corners anywhere in the home.

The house with no corners was built, and the Stickneys moved in. They held regular séances, often inviting friends over to participate. Life was good and things were going well until George Stickney was unexpectedly found dead in the home one day. His body was laying on the floor, ironically, in the only corner of the house. It's true. The builder had mistakenly included a regular corner in one of the rooms in the house. It was the only corner, and it would be where Mr. Stickney would spend his last moments alive.

No one has ever been able to figure out why Stickney happened to die in his least favorite place in the house. He was not fond of corners, so why would he have been standing in the only one that existed in the house? Perhaps, as the Stickneys believed was possible, a malevolent spirit had gotten trapped in the corner. Maybe, upon seeing the evil spirit, Stickney was literally scared to death.

Local folklore suggests the Stickney house is haunted, and old Stickney himself might be the one haunting it. After his ironic death, his wife Sylvia remained in the house where she claimed to still be in contact with her husband's ghost, as well as the ghosts of some of their children who had already passed on. The house became a popular place to visit among people wishing to make contact with a deceased loved one.

Sylvia Stickney often attracted quite a crowd when holding séances. Eventually, the house had other owners, although they would never be the sole occupants of the house without corners, as the Sticken eys seems to have stayed on. Mr. and Mrs. Stickney might still be haunting the house today. A strange figure can sometimes be seen on the stairs and another one looking out a window. The figure in the window has even been caught on camera.

In an interview with Chicago television station, WGN, a few years ago, a local police officer confirmed the rumors of strange sounds and unexplained events, like doors opening and closing independently or things being moved around on desks. He suggested the former Stickney Mansion that now hosts the local police department is haunted, possibly by the Stickneys themselves. Strange occurrences apparently happen quite regularly and shook the nerves of a few officers enough to seek other employment after experiencing too many disturbances themselves.

The Palmer House

The Stickney home is not the only haunted house in the northwestern suburbs. The Palmer House in Crystal Lake is also purported to be haunted. If you listen closely from outside the house, you will hear the muffled cries of children who sound as if they're being tortured. Put your ear to the front door and you might even hear some of the children clawing at it trying to get out.

So what could have happened in there? Legend has it the house was once an orphanage operated by a man named Palmer. Palmer allegedly tortured the children who lived there, sometimes beating them, and even murdering many of them. Even all these years later, the tormented spirits of the tortured children can still be heard haunting the Palmer house. And if you look closely, you can sometimes see their innocent faces peering through the basement windows as if trying to find a way out.

In addition to the Palmer House, several other areas of Crystal Lake are reputed to be haunted as well, and include a book store, two cemeteries, the YMCA, a park, and the Fountains of Crystal Lake. An old woman wanders the upper halls of the building overlooking the fountains and unidentified footsteps are often heard down in the building's basement.

The YMCA building is also believed to be haunted. Across the structure's parking lot lies a wooded area that once belonged to a farmer and his family. The farmer went mad one day and killed his entire family in the barn where wretched screams can still be heard today. The entire YMCA grounds are allegedly haunted.

The park in Covered Bridge Trails is also haunted, particularly around the small stream that runs through the park. Unusual orbs of light and mysterious shadows can be observed after dark.

The Barnes and Noble bookstore in Crystal Lake has also has its share of hauntings. Book carts mysteriously move on their own and other items are relocated without explanation. A ghostly elderly woman has also been seen in the back storeroom. Most people believe the woman who haunts the Barnes and Noble once owned the property long before it was commercialized. Legend has it she left her property to the church upon her death, but when it was sold off to developers, she practically rolled over in her grave and returned to haunt her precious land.

Finally, both the Lake View and Mount Thabor Cemeteries are home to hauntings. Glowing orbs of light, shadowy figures, and an odd green mist are just some of the bizarre things to have been observed at these two cemeteries.

All the hauntings in Crystal Lake have made it the perfect setting on which to base the *Friday the 13th* films in which Jason Voohries haunts the grounds of Camp Crystal Lake after drowning in a lake there. I wonder how the real ghosts of Crystal Lake would react to the somber spirit of Jason Voohries.

Handprints and Tracks

There are a number of stories circulating throughout the different suburbs of Chicago about stalled cars, train tracks, and children. In some cases, the story is told that a vehicle carrying several children stalled on the tracks and was subsequently hit by an oncoming train. Other versions tell of a lone child who was hit when wandering too close to some

Snow covered haunted railroad tracks. *Photo author's own*

tracks. Regardless of which version you hear, in all cases, when you stop your own vehicle on the tracks, it is almost always pushed across to safety by unseen hands. However, if you are resourceful enough to first sprinkle powder across your rear bumper you will sometimes see the small handprints of a child, or several children, after your vehicle was miraculously pushed out of harm's way.

For instance, somewhere in Bartlett, where the tracks cross Munger Road, a young boy was once run over by a passing train. It is sometimes possible to observe the tiny imprints of his hands on the trunk of your car if you sprinkle powder on it before pulling your vehicle onto the tracks and putting it in neutral.

An almost identical story is told in Belleville, where the train tracks are referred to as "the ghost tracks." In this case, another young boy will also push your car across the tracks to safety, only the tracks lay at the bottom of a sloped roadway and your car will be pushed back up the hill away from the tracks. The handprints of this boy can also be seen when any powdery substance is sprinkled across the back of the car.

In an undisclosed location in Kankakee, a bus full of children was once hit by a fast approaching train, killing everyone aboard. Ever since, children's laughter can be heard when crossing the tracks at night. If you can find this stretch of track, and you choose to park your car there and turn it off, you will hear a train in the distance quickly approaching, although no lights can ever be seen. Soon after, you'll feel your car being pushed over the tracks to the other side. Again, dusting your car with powder will enable your young saviors to leave a memento of their legacy.

Powis Road in Wayne, Illinois, features a mother and her children driving across the tracks when the car stalls. As the mother stands outside the vehicle trying to get it started again, a train comes. She is unable to rescue her children and they are all killed when the mammoth train plows right through the car. These children will also attempt to save you if your car is left on the tracks.

A similar story in Monmouth involves a school bus full of children going over a bridge and crashing to their deaths. As is the case with the railroad tracks, your car will be pushed to safety if left on the bridge. The children who died there sometimes leave handprints on your car windows, assuming you remembered to roll them up.

Getting back to the railroad tracks now, in Tolono, there is actually a "ghost train" that passes through every two weeks at about two in the morning. But in case you're thinking of waiting on the ghost train, it might be wise not to bother. Many people who have wandered down the tracks late at night, when no trains are scheduled to be on the tracks, have gone missing. Their mysterious disappearances always seem to coincide with the passing of the ghost train. Each time someone goes missing, the following week several signs with the person's picture and a message about how and when they first went missing can be seen posted in the area all around the tracks.

Finally, one of my favorite stories involving train tracks and hauntings occurred in Mundelein. There is a set of railroad tracks that passes over Hawley Street, that also happen to be just down the road from Carmel High School, a private Catholic school. Many of Carmel's students ride the train down those very tracks each morning on their way to school from some of the neighboring communities. The school is a short walk from the Mundelein train station. Many years ago the school was purported to conduct exorcisms on occasion. Most people thought it was all just gossip, until one student really seemed to be possessed. The efforts of several priests were not enough to exercise the boy's demons and he could not be saved. Shortly after their exorcism attempt, each one would suffer an untimely death, one of whom would die on the tracks when his car was hit by a train.

The possessed boy even died soon after the priests all died. The boy and the priests now haunt the area. The boy can be seen walking around the school grounds, and the priests are sometimes spotted on nights when there's a full moon. For years, Carmel High School students have been warned about the tracks, yet many of them continue to walk the long stretch of track from the platform to the intersection at Hawley Street on their way to and from the high school each day.

A few years ago, one unlucky boy walking the tracks failed to hear an approaching train when he was wearing headphones and listening to music. The boy was struck by the train and died. He still walks the tracks today but will never arrive at his intended destination.

Gurnee's Grotesque Iron Gate

Just as there are numerous versions of haunted crossings where train tracks and the road meet, there are also countless stories about haunted school houses and unspeakable horrors that befell the innocent children who once attended those schools. One of the most intriguing stories surrounds a heavy black iron gate that stands in Gurnee. The gate stands alone along a side road with an open field behind it. Years ago, the gate once marked the entrance to a school yard where a small schoolhouse stood. It was a happy place, and many of the local youngsters attended school there.

But one day, a heinous crime would be committed there. A demented man sauntered inside the schoolhouse and began killing all the children. The crazed man even cut the heads off of some of the children. In a grotesque gesture, the man placed several of the decapitated heads through the speared bars atop the gate. The community was understandably shaken by this monstrous offense and had the schoolhouse torn down. However, despite the absence of the schoolhouse, the gate still stands and the small heads of the children who lost their lives there are sometimes seen atop the gate, accompanied by the sad sounds of their sobbing.

Military Hauntings

Not far from Gurnee is the Great Lakes Naval Station and Recruit Training Command. Over the years, a number of strange stories have circulated about this place, not the least of which is that this is the real "Area 51" where extraterrestrial experiments are conducted in secret, while the deluded public mistakenly focuses their attention on the other Area 51 in Nevada. But never mind the aliens; we're here to hunt ghosts.

It seems there have been a number of deaths there over the years that have resulted in several hauntings. For instance, ship number fifteen caught fire years ago, killing many of the Navy recruits on board at the time. The perished recruits are said to now haunt the ship. Another recruit hung himself in ship number thirteen and can sometimes still be seen inside the ship. Interesting, he picked lucky number thirteen as the place where he would end his own life. Another spirit stalks the interior of ship twelve where an unidentified female is often heard screaming. It is best to be cautious if you are on the grounds at night, as dark figures regularly roam the naval station. Be especially wary of the ships, lest you be caught inside with a ghost.

The Haunted Hotel Near O'Hare

There is an eleven-story hotel in Rosemont, near O'Hare Airport, called the Sheraton Gateway Suites Hotel—and it's haunted. This haunted hotel is truly spooky. Guests have heard and seen dark figures walking through their rooms. There is no explanation for these occurrences. Each time a guest has observed someone in their room, the door was locked, so no one could have entered. Additionally, guests frequently hear noises emanating from inside the room that cannot possibly be coming from another guest's room. The entire hotel has soundproof walls to muffle the loud noise of airplanes flying in and out of the nearby O'Hare Airport. Any noises heard inside a guest's room are undoubtedly coming from that room.

On one occasion, a woman staying alone in the hotel hopped in the shower after ensuring the door to her room was locked and latched. When she walked out of the bathroom after showering she found all of her clothes sloppily tossed around the room. There have been countless reports of unearthly disturbances in the hotel. It seems the hotel has had a series of guests who never checked out. Multiple people have committed suicide by jumping from various balconies, one incident occurring as recently as 2001. A few other guests lost their lives in the hotel due to drug overdoses. Why this hotel has experienced so many deaths is unknown, but it's possible the ghosts that now haunt the hotel are constantly seeking eternal companions and might tempt guests to join them by jumping to their own deaths.

The Infamous Brown's Chicken Massacre of 1993

In the suburban town of Palatine, back in 1993, the Brown's Chicken and Pasta Restaurant became the site of a horrific slaying that left the place haunted for years to come. It was a frigid winter morning when police encountered a gruesome scene. Seven people had been murdered in cold blood, their bodies then stuffed into the freezers at the back of the restaurant. The restaurant had been robbed and all the witnesses killed.

The restaurant was immediately shut down and remained empty for a full year before another business would occupy the place. Throughout the time the building stood vacant, strange sounds could be heard coming from inside that would continue even after the building was eventually occupied by a dry cleaning business. Gunshots and screams were sometimes heard there, and sudden temperature changes often occurred without explanation. The dry cleaning business remained in the building for a few years before finally going out of business, after which time the building was demolished.

However, residents of the area still reported hearing unexplained noises coming from the site of the slayings. Finally, in 2002, two men were arrested and charged with the seven grisly murders that had been executed in the Brown's Chicken Restaurant almost a decade earlier. Following the arrests of those two individuals, things seemed to quiet down and the spirits of the seven victims could finally rest in peace.

The Bartonville Insane Asylum and other Haunted Psych Wards

Moving on from the northern suburbs, there are just as many haunted hot spots in the southern portion of the state. Not the least of which is the Peoria State Hospital for the Incurable Insane in Bartonville, Illinois. The institution is no longer in operation, and hasn't been for several decades. But just because there's been limited human activity since the hospital closed down in the 1970s, doesn't mean there aren't other things going on there.

A quick look around the abandoned hospital building and nearby cemetery is enough to convince anyone that an aberrant presence exists there. Over the years, tons of trespassers have tested their fortitude by braving the creepy trek around the hospital grounds. Each time, they come back thoroughly spooked by the many strange sights and sounds going on there. But in all the stories of hauntings at the asylum, there is one paranormal presence that stands out most and has come to characterize the old hospital, giving it a name and a face.

Back when the hospital was still in operation, whenever any of the patients passed on, the deceased were buried in the hospital's cemetery. There weren't necessarily many onlookers, mostly just hospital staff and sometimes other patients. One patient, by the name of Bookbinder, took it upon himself to attend every burial. Each time was the same. Bookbinder always stood in the same familiar spot leaning against a nearby elm tree, and every time he cried vociferously. It didn't matter that he sometimes never even knew the person being buried. Bookbinder stood respectfully at every burial, and always by the same elm tree. That was until his own burial.

The staff loved Bookbinder's outgoing personality, so when he died, they all came to the cemetery to pay their respects the day he was to be buried. After paying homage to Bookbinder, it was time to say goodbye and lower his casket into the grave. But just as the casket was being lowered downward, the sound of loud sobbing could be heard coming from the elm tree where Bookbinder always stood during burial ceremonies. When everyone turned to look toward the tree, there was Bookbinder leaning against it like always. No one could believe their eyes, of course, and the casket was opened. There inside was Bookbinder resting peacefully. Just as quickly as they had confirmed Bookbinder was inside the casket, the apparition that had been seen by the tree disappeared.

Interestingly enough, not long after Bookbinder's body had been laid to rest, the old elm tree withered and died. Rather than leave the dead tree standing among the graves, hospital staff decided to chop it down, but when the first swing of the axe splintered the tree's bark, a load moaning sound could be heard coming from the tree. It was so frightful, that the tree was spared momentarily. Instead of chopping it down, a decision was made to burn the dead tree. It was set on fire, and a few staff members watched it become engulfed in flames. When the tree was completely ablaze, an eerie moaning sound could be heard emanating from it. The cries were of someone in pain and they seemed to be coming from the tree. Those who stood witness couldn't stand the unexplained moaning and quickly quelled the fire. That would be the last time anyone attempted to destroy the tree. Although the hospital cemetery might appear desolate these days, should you ever find yourself there, take a closer look and listen for Bookbinder who still haunts the place.

The old asylum in Bartonville isn't the only haunted hospital in the Chicago suburbs. Many of the former psychiatric hospitals that used to be in operation were known to perform bizarre experiments and procedures on their patients in years past. Many people believe those patients now haunt the hospitals where they were once tortured, and continue to haunt the sites even after the hospitals have been closed down or demolished. There are a handful of these places, including: the Choate Mental Health Center and the Elgin State Mental Hospital.

The Choate Mental Health Center once stood in Anna, Illinois, but was burned to the ground years ago. All that remains there now are the basements of the various hospital buildings and the tunnels that connected them to one another. After the hospital had closed for good, and before the buildings ever burned down, there were reports of hauntings there. Shadowy figures could be seen roaming around the property, and strange faces sometimes peered out from the windows of the various buildings. One daring gentleman even ventured inside to have a look around, and when he made his way down to the tunnels, he felt a hand touch his back despite no one else being there with him. On another occasion, a curiosity seeker was attacked by a phantom dog in one of the old patient's rooms. This unlucky individual bore the scratches to prove it, but there was never any dog found in the building. The buildings were believed to be haunted by former patients and staff members. Even after the buildings were gone, people still reported strange happenings in the area. Perhaps a few restless spirits still wander the underground tunnels that ran beneath the once erect mental hospital.

The Elgin State Mental Hospital was another site where invasive therapy methods, like electroshock therapy, were performed on patients. This was largely a phenomenon of the 1950s. Treatment methods could be so cruel that many patients died as a result. The hospital had its own cemetery where deceased patients were buried, but eventually the cemetery became too crowded and no more bodies could be buried there. Instead, many of them were cremated in the basement incinerator. It all sounds a bit barbaric, and the merciless manner in which so many of the patients died may have prevented their poor souls from ever attaining peace.

Long after the hospital was finally shut down, trespassers reported hearing strange screams and sometimes observed shadowy figures and unexplained fog inside the building, as well as lights turning on and off independently. Some of the interior walls were speckled in blood and the entire place reeked of death. For years, unexplained disturbances plagued the empty hospital until it was torn down after it was discovered to have asbestos.

Additional paranormal activity has also been experienced in the hospital cemetery. An unsettling rumor regarding the cemetery posits that as the cemetery became full, bodies were stacked as many as five high, with only the name of the topmost body appearing on the grave marker. Unusual sights and sounds have been experienced in the cemetery, but the most notable is the perpetual occurrence of visitors clumsily dropping objects on the ground at night and not being able to find them, despite having a flashlight to illuminate the area. Whenever anyone returns the following day, the missing items are always discovered sitting atop the headstones, as if someone gently placed them there. Perhaps it is the ghosts' way of ensuring someone will always return to keep them company.

Raggedy Ann's Revenge

In Mattoon, Illinois, sits a haunted cemetery just beyond the Coles County Airport. The unusual thing about this haunting is that it is not necessarily the restless spirit of a deceased person doing the haunting. In this case, it is that of a doll. The doll belonged to a nine-year-old girl who used to carry it with her everywhere. The doll was a rag doll with red hair and a blue dress, much like the popular Raggedy Ann and Andy dolls, and may have actually been a Raggedy Ann doll, but that detail is a bit sketchy. The little girl loved that doll. It was her loyal companion. But in a single moment, the days of the little girl and her rag doll playing side by side would be over.

An unidentified intruder forced his way into the family's home and killed the young girl. The man has never been caught and the case has gone cold as far as authorities are concerned. However, there is one restless entity that refuses to forget. The girl's parents had buried her with her beloved doll. Legend has it that the doll is out for revenge. On certain nights, if you are brave enough to venture into the cemetery, you can sometimes see the rag doll hanging by its neck from the large tree that stands over the murdered girl's grave. The rag doll normally does not appear until around midnight and remains hanging until morning, when it disappears with the light of day. Who knows why it is the doll that haunts and not the little girl. But one thing is for certain: With the little rag doll on the loose, it would seem there might be something to all those Chucky movies after all.

The Haunted House of Frank Shaver Allen

The Frank Shaver Allen house in Joliet, at the corner of Morgan and Dewey, has been known to be haunted for the past several decades. There was even a big hoopla over the haunting back in the 1970s, when a team of psychics was assembled to investigate the alleged hauntings. The story was covered by newspaper reporters and made headlines. Following their inspection of the home, the team of psychics concluded that the house was indeed plagued by paranormal activity.

The family occupying the house at the time had been experiencing unusual disturbances for more than ten years. Handymen, gas meter readers, and other guests even observed supernatural phenomena in and around the home. Doors opened and closed on their own, strange odors emanated from within, dark ghostly figures meandered through the house, and several unidentified voices and screams were also heard on multiple occasions. There was even a rash of unexplained phantom fires.

The paranormal investigation conducted by the psychic team revealed who some of the spirits haunting that house might be. The home was originally constructed in the late 1800s for the Frank Shaver Allen family. It is believed that Frank Shaver Allen himself now haunts the house, along with several ghostly companions. A nanny and a young boy are sometimes seen together in the house. At the time, a young boy also lived in the home, and was often visited by the specter boy who tried tempting the young boy to join him as his playmate for eternity. An elderly woman, who died from a terminal illness in the home, has also been spotted there. These are the most commonly reported spirits seen lingering in the house, but there are many others. If you were looking for a real life haunted house, this is it.

The Watseka Possessions

Stories of possessions have petrified people forever. Movie makers have capitalized on this fear, producing such films as *The Exorcist* and *The Exorcism of Emily Rose*. But what we often forget when watching these movies is that they are based on real-life events. What's even more interesting is that young girls always seem to be the target of these possessions. Some survive the ordeal while others aren't so lucky. And for a few the experience is ephemeral. But for the rest, they suffer persistent domination of their souls by restless spirits.

In the 1860s and 70s, the small town of Watseka, south of the city, witnessed the possession of two young girls born years apart. And even more amazing was the phenomenon that the first girl to be possessed would later inhabit the body of the second girl to also become possessed. The Roff family lived in Watseka for several years before the Vennum family would move there. Once the Vennum's did move to Watseka, they would not meet the Roff's until after discovering they both shared a daughter. The Vennum's had a thirteen-year-old daughter named Lurancy who, soon after moving to Watseka, would become acquainted with the Roff's daughter, Mary. The only catch was that Mary had died in 1865, when Lurancy was only a year old.

Lurancy began exhibiting some extremely bizarre behavior, such as slipping into long lasting trances and speaking in a variety of voices and languages. As Lurancy's behavior became increasingly aberrant, her parents consulted several doctors who recommended she be institutionalized at the state mental hospital in Peoria (Peoria State Hospital for the Incurable Insane), a place that would later become haunted itself.

Lurancy's parents were seriously considering the doctors' recommendation when they received an unexpected visitor who would change their minds. Mr. Roff came calling when he heard about the Vennum daughter's condition. It distinctly reminded him of his own daughter, Mary, who had died years earlier.

When Mary Roff was still alive she displayed many of the same behaviors Lurancy was now exhibiting. At the time, no one could determine what was wrong with her, so she was labeled as insane and sent to an asylum where she would be tortured by the barbaric experimental treatment methods used at that time. Mary regularly tried to bleed herself in order to flush out the demons that haunted her. Mary's father always suspected spirits were inhabiting her body, but he was helpless to alleviate her suffering. When she almost died trying to bleed herself out, he finally gave up and reluctantly admitted her to the state mental hospital where she later died.

Years after Mary Roff's death, an identical situation would occur in the very same town. Mary's father became convinced that young Lurancy Vennum had been possessed by spirits, both good and bad. Everyone thought his theory preposterous, until Lurancy claimed to be possessed by the spirit of Roff's own daughter, Mary. Amazingly, Lurancy began divulging information about the Roff family that only Mary Roff could have known, things that had occurred before Lurancy was even born.

As Lurancy's condition worsened, she became increasingly distant from her family and wanted to go with the Roff's. The Vennom's finally succumbed and permitted their beloved daughter to leave and live with the Roff's. Lurancy lived with the Roff family as Mary, and she seemed quite happy there, but she always advised them that she could not stay long. Life went on this way for several months, and then Mary said goodbye and left her family behind. Lurancy had returned and the Vennums were relieved. The funny thing is Lurancy had no recollection of the many months during which she lived with the Roff family as Mary. Lurancy went on to live a normal life and had a family of her own, and as far as anyone knows, she was never possessed by the spirit of Mary or anyone else ever again.

Folklore & Legends

C hicago is rich in folklore, and in addition to all the great ghost stories and haunted hot spots around the city, there are also many well known legends. Most of these legends have been circulating for years, although one local legend is quite recent. You may have even witnessed it yourself, the appearance of the Virgin Mary. Some of the other legends you might have heard growing up. The stories have all become part of the culture of Chicago and are simultaneously cherished and feared by all those who are familiar. These legends are the stuff of scary sleepovers sitting in a circle with your friends chanting "light as a feather, stiff as a board," or late nights home alone standing in front of the bathroom mirror in the dark calling out to Bloody Mary or the Candy Man. These are the stories that both fascinate and terrify you. You're hooked as the story is being told and it all seems relatively benign until you find yourself alone in the dark with odd noises emanating from all around. And then, as a chill runs down your spine, you begin to wonder if the legends are real.

The Legend of La Llorona

The weeping woman known as La Llorona ("lah yoh-ROH-nah") wanders along rivers looking for her lost children. Night after night this poor woman roams the earth in a long white gown trying to find her innocent children, who have been missing forever. As she travels from place to place, you can sometimes hear her calling out to them, "Ay, mis hijos!" (Oh, my children). La Llorona seems condemned to a lonely existence without her beloved babies. It is truly heartbreaking. But before you feel too sorry for this lamenting lady you should probably hear the whole story.

Beware of the weeping lady along the river. *Photo author's own*

La Llorona is not content to simply search for her children. She seems to want others to suffer just as she does. And because she cannot find her own kids, La Llorona sometimes snatches other children from their homes during the night. Her cries should be heeded as a warning because if you hear her, she just might be coming for you. And when she finds you, she is likely to kill you.

So where are La Llorona's children and why does she search the rivers for them? Well, the last time La Llorona saw her children alive was in a river near their home, but they weren't swimming. La Llorona had gone mad and dragged them down to the river and drowned them. After the veil of madness had lifted, La Llorona realized what she had done and tried to pull her children from the river, but it was too late. They had been washed away with the current and she could not find them. She searched all night to no avail. They were gone. Their tiny bodies would never be found. But La Llorona is relentless and continues to search in every river and lake she encounters, hoping to finally find her lost children. Late at night you can sometimes hear her mournful sobbing off in the distance, and it's enough to make your hairs stand on end. And if you do hear her, you'd better hope you don't become her next victim. Her cries resound like a banshee warning of an impending death. She most often comes for children, but is said to slay young and old alike. And unlike other apparitions who are bound to a particular location, often the site of their deaths or their final resting place, La Llorona's wandering ways allow her to roam without limits. So watch out if you live near a river or a lake, because you never know when she might be in your neck of the woods.

The legend of La Llorona has been passed on from parents to children for generations, primarily among Hispanic and Latino families. The legend of La Llorona originally began in Central and South American countries, but has made its way north to Chicago where it is now widely told throughout the city and surrounding areas. It is a popular story, most often shared by parents with their young children. Children are advised that it is unwise to be out after dark and are warned to get to bed early to avoid being snatched away by La Llorona. She is not known to disturb sleeping children, but watch out if she catches them outside late at night. She is likely to drag them off and drown them.

There are numerous explanations as to why La Llorona drowned her poor children. The saddest account is one that involves heartbreak and betrayal. La Llorona was a beautiful woman who was always noticed wherever she went. She came from a poor family, so when she fell in love with a wealthy man they had to keep their relationship secret, as the upper echelons with whom he normally associated would not have approved. The man made her many promises, especially after she had his two children, both boys. Unfortunately, their love would not last, and the man would become betrothed to another. Some say he forsook his love for someone of his same social standing. Whether it was by choice, or through an arranged marriage, he left La Llorona broken hearted and alone to raise two young reminders of the man she had loved but who had abandoned her.

One evening when La Llorona was out walking with her children on a path that ran along the river, a carriage passed by. When the gentleman driving the carriage realized the two boys were his own, he stopped to speak with them but ignored La Llorona. He was seated next to an elegant young woman, surely his new bride for whom he had abandoned La Llorona. As she continued observing her former lover and his wife interacting with her children, the hurt she felt inside began to twist into an insane obsession. Once the carriage departed, La Llorona would commit an unspeakable act. She would murder her own children, drowning them in the heavy waters of the river. When she would finally come to her senses, it would be too late to save them.

Another version of the La Llorona legend depicts her as someone with much more selfish motivation. Some people say that La Llorona used to neglect her small children to go out at night, seeking attention from adoring men who were easily charmed by her. She is said to have loved all the attention, but of course, having two young children at home wasn't easy. She spent night after night out dancing and socializing with the men of the area. One night, after returning from another evening out, La Llorona found her children to be missing. Their fragile bodies were discovered drowned in the river the following morning. Generous accounts of what happened suggest the boys wandered off in their mother's absence and drowned on their own accidentally. However, a more sinister story describes La Llorona as a murderous mother who cold heartedly drowned her own children so that she could be free to fraternize with all her gentlemen admirers.

Regardless of the version you believe, La Llorona's plight is always the same. She is destined to wander the earth, weeping and wailing, in search of her dead children. When she had first killed her children, she continued to look for their missing bodies that had washed downstream and were never seen again. It is presumed that she died herself while looking for them.

Upon her death, she was confronted by God, who asked her where her children were. Each time he asked, she only answered that she did not know and would not admit to what she had done. As punishment for her heinous act and subsequent failure to admit to it, she was ordered to spend eternity looking for her lost children. She will not enter the gates of heaven until she finds her children and brings them before the Lord. So from now until the end of time, La Llorona will continue to traverse the globe checking all the rivers and lakes she comes across.

She often attempts to replace her own children by snatching other innocent children she meets when out wandering. Those poor children she steals will suffer the same inevitable fate as her own children did. She drowns them and then attempts to present them as her own before God who, of course, cannot be fooled. So La Llorona continues to wander the earth crying, and unsuspecting children continue to go missing. Don't think La Llorona comes only after the children, though. Anyone who dares seek her presence might soon find themselves facing a fatal end as she does not like to be looked in the face and will kill you, if you do so.

El Duende

La Llorona is not the only legend of Latin origin to be shared by families in the Chicago area. There is a strange story of El Duende, a short troll like man with backward feet that will haunt you for life if you're unlucky enough to be visited by him. The legend of El Duende first began circulating in various Central and South American countries, including Guatemala for instance, and then, followed immigrating families to the Chicago area. El Duende was a fallen angel who was thrown out of heaven for carrying envy toward God. He has a nasty mean streak and enjoys playing pranks on people, but most often targets young ladies.

El Duende would appear unexpectedly to young unmarried women, particularly while they bathed in the warm river waters running near their villages. The young girls would wait until the more discrete evening hours when the sun was soon setting to walk down to the river and bathe. They would not notice the odd little man hiding in the trees waiting for them. At first it would seem that the innocent young girls had only to fear being peeped at by the mysterious short man. But a glimpse of El Duende would result in something far more lasting than the mild embarrassment of being seen in the buff while bathing. It seems soon after spotting El Duende, young women begin experiencing a host of bizarre occurrences. They suffer unexplained black outs and horrible nightmares as El Duende starts following them, popping up in unexpected places. The worst part of

Watch out for El Duende up in the trees. *Photo courtesy of Christina Matyskela*

El Duende's legacy is that the unlucky young ladies who see him, and are subsequently followed by him, will never have another boyfriend, and will never be married for their entire lives. El Duende drives away unsuspecting potential suitors, so that these women essentially become betrothed only to him, if only because of his persistent haunting.

In time, many of these women begin to exhibit slight signs of madness, as El Duende continues to haunt them. There are even accounts of El Duende following women from their South American homes to destinations as far away as Chicago in an effort to escape him.

As the legend has made its way to Chicago, El Duende has been known to visit young women just as they are about to shower. Many young women have so feared the El Duende that they've cut their long hair short to throw him off, as he only seeks out young ladies with long locks. El Duende is a peculiar creature and should be avoided at all costs.

The Candy Man

Who can make you scream and cry? Who can make your day go awry? The Candy Man can, the Candy Man can...

The Candy Man is something of a celebrity. In 1992, an entire movie was made about him. The Candy Man can be found in Chicago's sprawling public housing project, the largest and most infamous in the nation, Cabrini Green. He haunts one of the dismal drug-infested project buildings where, in an abandoned apartment on the uppermost floor, he painted a graphic mural depicting the earthly fate that would immortalize him in the minds of Cabrini residents forever.

The Candy Man, as he would come to be called later, lived sometime during the days of slavery in the 1800s. But despite his lowly plot in life, the Candy Man had developed an artistic ability and loved to paint. He also found himself in love with a beautiful young woman who would become pregnant with his child. What could be better than that? It should have been a blessed time, but there was one problem. The Candy Man was a slave and a black man, and the love of his life, pregnant with his child, was the white daughter of a plantation owner. The Candy Man would be hunted and tortured for his audacious attempt at seducing a white woman. It didn't matter that the relationship was consensual. He was black and that was all that mattered. The young black artist would suffer a horrific death. First, after having been beaten to near death, the very hand he used to express his artistic visions on canvas was crudely sawn off. Then, as he lie there dripping in blood, his attackers poured sticky sweet honey all over him and watched as swarms of hostile bees continued stinging the "Candy Man" until he sighed his last breath and died.

The Candy Man now wears a hook where his artist's hand had once been and is often seen shrouded in hordes of bees. He waits for those intrigued enough to invite him forth by calling his name. Legend has it that if you stand in front of the mirror and call his name five times consecutively he will appear before you. Make no mistake about it. He will kill you. He'll slash you open, gutting you with his hook hand. With each victim he kills, his legend grows and he lives on long after his own brutal death more than a century ago, which occurred in the area that is now Cabrini Green, a place known for gangs, drugs, and extreme violence. Perhaps the entire area is cursed by the violent nature of the Candy Man's death.

The Candy Man's story has persisted for a time, but that time might be up very soon. With city plans for urban renewal and the construction of several experimental mixed income condominiums, many of Chicago's Cabrini Green housing projects have been demolished. So what will happen to the Candy Man? Will his legend fade or will he continue to haunt the developing new neighborhoods? Only time will tell.

The Virgin Mary

A more recent phenomenon that will surely contribute to local legend, as the story is told to future generations, is the appearance of the Virgin Mary on the Fullerton Road underpass of the I-94 expressway. As flowers began blooming in the spring of 2006, something miraculous would emerge at an expressway underpass. What was believed to be a salt stain on the cement wall of the I-94 underpass at Fullerton Road amazingly appeared in the image of the Virgin Mary. It is unclear who first discovered the vision, but once revealed Chicagoans would flock to the underpass in large numbers. People lined up for blocks to get a glimpse of the holy image. Traffic along Fullerton Road backed up regularly as onlookers slowed to observe the image of the Virgin Mary. It was undeniable just how distinctly the "stain" resembled the Virgin Mary.

The story became quite large in Chicago, as local news crews continued to report on the events of the Fullerton/I-94 underpass. As the story gained appeal and the number of daily visitors grew exponentially, the city decided to take control of the situation after one gentleman decided to write "Big Lie" above the image. The Illinois Department of Transportation (IDOT) decided to paint over the image in order to discourage any further activity at the spot. Others defaced the wall by adding graffiti over the IDOT paint job.

But to everyone's amazement, the Virgin Mary returned, although she had a little help. It seems two devout Catholic women took it upon themselves to wash the paint and graffiti from the beloved Virgin Mary. In years to come, the triumphant return of the Virgin Mary is sure to be told a bit differently. Certain details of the story will likely be excluded so that there will never have been anyone who cleaned the Virgin. She will have reappeared as a true sign from God.

Regardless, her initial appearance was amazing enough. The image bore more than a striking resemble to the Virgin Mary. It was the Virgin Mary. Why she chose to appear in that spot will never be known or understood, but religious Chicagoans will forever feel blessed to have been honored by her presence.

Bloody Mary

From the Virgin Mary to Bloody Mary, our story takes a twist and we move on to scarier sightings. Young people around Chicago have been telling the story of Bloody Mary to one another for years. Bloody Mary often refers to a sort of game, but it is more than just a simple game, as it is intended to summon an apparition—that of Bloody Mary. Anyone can do it. Wait until nightfall. Then go stand in front of the bathroom mirror, much like you would calling for the Candy Man. While standing there in the dark staring intently at your own reflection in the mirror, repeat her name three times. "Bloody Mary, Bloody Mary, Bloody Mary." If you're lucky, you'll see her image in your reflection. In your face you will see hers, scarred, cut and bloody. If you're unlucky, she'll actually appear next to you and try to kill you by viciously ripping your face right off.

The game often becomes one of bravery, as most who try are too timid to get past the second "Bloody Mary." It is also possible to see your future revealed before your eyes, but there's a huge risk in calling her name for that end, as she might just slash your face. Some people believe that she will occasionally choose to reveal the summoner's future concerning marriage and children.

There is a lot of speculation about who Bloody Mary really was, but no one knows for sure. Some people even doubt her existence, but are you willing to take that risk and call out to her, or will you hesitate before repeating Bloody Mary's name on the third time?

The Cursed Cubs

Legend has it the Chicago Cubs are cursed and have been for more than half a century. They haven't made it to the World Series since 1945, and it's been nearly 100 years since they won the pennant back in 1908. The Chicago Cubs have long suffered a series of losing seasons. They just can't seem to get it together. Further, after leaving to sign with other teams, many former Cubs players go on to have winning seasons with their new teams, even making it to the playoffs. On the flip side, teams that have recruited too many former Cubs players have subsequently experienced major losing streaks. So are the Cubs cursed?

The curse of the Cubs has long been part of Chicago history. Some might scoff at talk of a curse, but there's no denying a mystical malady of some sort has plagued the Chicago Cubbies for far too long. For those who don't know, they might mistakenly assume that an expression like "we're cursed" is

Wrigley Field, home of the cursed Cubs. *Photo author's own*

just a figure of speech. But the Cubs are cursed, and have been since 1945, when they last played in the World Series.

A curse was placed on the Cubs by a frustrated fan attending game four of the 1945 World Series, which took place in Chicago. The fan's name was Billy Sianis and he had purchased two tickets to that fateful game. But it wouldn't be a family member or friend who would accompany old Billy to the game. Billy, it seems, preferred the company of a "billy" goat. It's true. Billy Sianis brought his pet goat to the game. Accounts differ as to what actually transpired that day, but the gist of it is that Billy or his goat somehow angered security staff who subsequently kicked Billy and his goat out of the stadium. Apparently, the goat wasn't smelling his best that day. Mr. Sianis took great offense to the whole fiasco and yelled to Cubs owner Philip Knight Wrigley that he would curse the Cubs from that day forward so that they would never win another pennant or play in a World Series at Wrigley Field ever again. That was back in 1945, and they haven't made it to the World Series since.

Over the years there have been several attempts to lift the curse by parading goats around the stadium, but nothing has had any lasting effect. The Cubs might win for a while, but eventually things always end the same way—the Cubs lose. Relatives of the now deceased Billy Sianis have advised Cubs officials to stop dragging goats into the stadium simply for publicity or to break the curse. Until the Cubs Organization legitimately and sincerely develops an affinity for goats, the curse will continue. Keep trying Cubbies!

That's All She Wrote Folks

It's been a long and haunted road but we finally made it to the end. Chicago is an interesting city whether you believe in ghosts or not, but its supernatural side certainly lends an additional element of excitement. For the curiosity seekers out there, wondering where to find all these places, many of those mentioned here are easily found with a quick check of the map, some a bit more obscure, although I have elected not to include specific locations or directions in the book. The focus here has been in the telling of the tale. In doing so, I hope you found yourself a little more frightened of the dark, maybe even feeling your heart skip a beat at every bump in the night.

People have long been fascinated by that which cannot be explained, from ghosts to aliens, and even the world's many ancient wonders. The idea of ghosts is especially intriguing since it suggests there is something more for us after this life. It means also that we'll be reunited with those who have gone before us. And though we often fear the unknown, we also chase after it. We want to see those spirits, no matter how scared we might be. And if we should encounter an apparition, the experience would undoubtedly be exhilarating, albeit terrifying. Ghost stories have become entwined in our collective psyche, and no where is that more true than in the bustling city of Chicago. The city of Chicago is legendary in and of itself, and its true ghost stories only enhance its celebrated status. Chicago will remain one of the country's greatest cities for years to come, as well as one of its most haunted.

Bibliography

Addams, Jane. *The Second Twenty Years at Hull House.* New York, New York: MacMillan Press, 1930; Boondocks Edition, 2000.

Bielski, Ursula. *Creepy Chicago: A Ghosthunter's Tales of the City's Scariest Sites.* Chicago, Illinois: Lake Claremont Press, 2003.

Bielski, Ursula. *More Chicago Haunts: Scenes from Myth and Memory.* Chicago, Illinois: Lake Claremont Press, 2000.

Bielski, Ursula. *Chicago Haunts: Ghostlore of the Windy City.* Chicago, Illinois: Lake Claremont Press, 1998.

Cahill, Tim. *Buried Dreams: Inside the Mind of a Serial Killer.* New York, New York: Bantam Books, 1986.

Chicago Historical Society. *A Basic Chronology of Chicago History: Transportation, Commerce, Communication, and Population.* Chicago, Illinois: Department of Education and Public Programs, 1985.

Crowe, Richard T. *Chicago Street Guide to the Supernatural: A Guide to Haunted and Legendary Places in and Near the Windy City*. Oak Park, Illinois: Carolando Press, 2000.

Facchini, Rocco A., and Facchini, Daniel J. *Muldoon: A True Chicago Ghost Story. Tales of a Forgotten Rectory*. Chicago, Illinois: Lake Claremont Press, 2003.

Falsani, Cathleen. *Ghost Book Popular Among Priests*. Chicago, Illinois: Chicago Sun-Times, January 11, 2004.

Fanjul, Juan Carlos. *Stickney Mansion*. Chicago, Illinois: WGN News Cover Story, October 31, 2005.

Graczyk, Jim. *Field Guide to Chicago Hauntings*. Oak Lawn, Illinois: Ghost Research Society Press, 2006.

Hauck, Dennis W. *Haunted Places, The National Directory: A Guidebook to Ghostly Abodes, Sacred Sites, UFO Landings, and other Supernatural Locations*. New York, New York: Penguin Books, 1996.

Hayes, Joe. *La Llorona, The Weeping Woman: An Hispanic Legend told in Spanish and English*. El Paso, Texas: Cinco Puntos Press, 2004.

Kaczmarek, Dale. *Windy City Ghosts 2*. Alton, Illinois: Whitechapel Productions Press, 2001.

Kaczmarek, Dale. *Windy City Ghosts*. Alton, Illinois: Whitechapel Productions Press, 2000.

Lasswell, David. *The Chicago Fire*. Chicago, Illinois: Chicago Historical Society, 1971.

Lindberg, Richard. *Return to the Scene of the Crime: A Guide to Infamous Places in Chicago*. Nashville, Tennessee: Cumberland House, 2001.

Malden, Joyce, and Municipal Reference Collection Staff. *Historical Information about Chicago*. Chicago, Illinois: Chicago Public Library, 1975.

Oboler, Suzanne, and Gonzalez, Deena J. *The Oxford Encyclopedia of Latinos and Latinas in the United States*. Oxford, New York: Oxford University Press: 2005.

Pohlen, Jerome. *Oddball Illinois: A Guide to Some Really Strange Places*. Chicago, Illinois: Chicago Review Press, 2000.

Riccio, Dolores, and Bingham, Joan. *Haunted Houses USA*. New York, New York: Pocket Books, 1989.

Scott, Beth, and Normal, Michael. *Haunted Heartland*. New York, New York: Warner Books, 1985.

St. Clair, David. *Watseka*. Chicago, Illinois: Playboy Press, 1977.

Taylor, Troy. *Haunted Chicago: History & Hauntings of the Windy City*. Chicago, Illinois: Whitechapel Productions Press, 2003.

Taylor, Troy. *Haunted Illinois*. Alton, Illinois: Whitechapel Productions Press, 1999.

Unsworth, Tim. *Stuck in a Rectory with a Curmudgeon and a Bishop's Ghost*. Chicago, Illinois: National Catholic Reporter, March 29, 2002.

Index

Exorcism of Emily Rose, the, 133
Exorcist, the, 133

F

Flapper Ghost, 50-51
Frank Shaver Allen house, 132-133
Friday the 13th, 121

G

George Pullman, 73
German Church Road, 101-104
Ghost in the Graveyard, 57
Givens Mansion, 33
Graceland Cemetery, 73-74
Great Fire of 1871, 21, 24
Great Lakes Naval Station, 126
Grimes Sisters, 102-105
Gurnee, 125

H

Harpo Studios, 18-19
Herman Webster Mudgett, 88, 92
Holy Sepulcher Cemetery, 78
House of Weird Death, 106
Hull House, 29-33

I

Inez Clarke, 73-74
Irish Castle, 33
Iroquois Theater, 25-29
Italian Bride, 78-79